Advance Praise

Sherri Shunfenthal believes deeply in the power of spirituality to transform one's life. As a Rabbi, I sometimes wrestle with ways in which to help people feel the warmth and excitement of various Jewish celebrations. Reading these poems enhances my connection to our Festivals and Life Cycle occasions. Sherri's poems capture the depth and joy that these sacred occasions are meant to facilitate. When Sherri writes about Shabbat, memories of her mother, a wedding, or Festival poems, her writing reaches into the heart. Sherri often speaks of 'reaching' in her poems. I hope these poems will help the reader reach closer to the Divine in their lives.

-Rabbi Bruce Aft, Congregation Adat Reyim, Springfield, Virginia

Sherri asked me to read and review her new book of poems, *Seasons of Prayer* right before I was heading off for a "sibling reunion" in Tucson, AZ . It also was the day before the beginning of Passover. I took her manuscript with me and decided to begin by reading the section on "Passover." When I gathered with my three siblings and their spouses, I told them I wanted to start our time together reading a poem by Sherri Shunfenthal called "Remembering Our Stories at Passover." As Sherri says in her Notes to Readers the poems "are great opening for discussion," and this one was perfect to begin sharing our stories of the past two years.

Like telling stories these poems are imaginative insightful words to help us uniquely and creatively to encounter every special occasion and tradition of the Jewish year. At the 9/11/01 interfaith prayer service the shofar was sounded and it was *"piercing the air like a cry ...the shofar sounds, declares and punctuates, draws us together...a symbol of rescue."* My whole being remembered and said "Yes" when I read these words of the poem, "The Shofar Sounds."

Thank you Sherri for giving us poetry perspective to make the seasons of worship traditions fresh and new and inspiring. *"She (Miriam) followed Moses across the Red Sea that opened like a woman's womb to give birth to her people. Miriam the midwife delivered the mothers of Israel safely across then sang to her newborn children, praises to G-d."* From "Miriam's Faith" - Beautiful!

-Reverend Dr. Beth Braxton

I've always loved Sherri Waas Shunfenthal's poetry. Her verses invariably speak from the heart to the heart. And her newest collection, *Seasons of Prayer*, is no exception. Sherri's approach to the Jewish year is insightful and thoughtful. Even if you're a relative newcomer to Jewish holidays and observances, you will find something in Sherri's poetry that resonates with you. You will marvel at her ability to capture and encapsulate the emotional moments that arise during the year. I often refer to Sherri's poems when I am looking for interesting approaches to the Jewish cycle of life, and I'm sure you will, too.

-Cantor George Henschel, Kol HaLev Synagogue
Community, Baltimore, MD

Seasons of Prayer

Sherri Waas Shunfenthal

Pocol Press

Clifton, VA

POCOL PRESS
Published in the United States of America
by Pocol Press
6023 Pocol Drive
Clifton, VA 20124
www.pocolpress.com

Publisher's Cataloguing-in-Publication

Shunfenthal, Sherri Waas.

    Seasons of prayer / Sherri Waas Shunfenthal.
    p. cm.
    ISBN: 978-1-929763-61-0

1. Spiritual life--Judaism. 2. Jewish religious poetry. English.

3. Prayers. 4. Meditation--Judaism—Poetry. I. Title.

    BM723S578 2014

    296.7/2--dc23   2014949659

Library of Congress Control Number: 2014949659

Cover and interior art by Jennifer Shunfenthal.

Cover art graphic assistance provided by Amelia Hetrick.

Dedication

This book is dedicated to my loving family and friends.

And to the loving memory of my mom who encouraged and inspired me to write poetry.

Introduction

I imagine poems as paper airplanes. They fly through the air and land right where they are meant to be. Readers often find a phrase, idea or thought that has special significance to them, then read it over and over.

Poetry has the ability to capture ideas and thoughts in simple, meaningful ways. Poetry can open us and help us see with new eyes. As I've written and revised poems, I was inspired to realize that Judaism has seasons of holidays that center around the opportunity for renewal, reflection, hope and re-awakening. As nature follows cycles and rhythms, Jewish holidays follow the cycles and rhythms of seasons and life. There is a daily cycle, a weekly cycle, monthly and yearly cycle of prayer. New Year celebrates the beginning of time. We start the reading of Torah at Simchat Torah and follow through to completion at the end of the year. Jewish holidays follow the same rhythm and cycle each year. They are as dependable as changing colors of autumn leaves and yet leave us open for renewal and refreshing our spirit.

There is a cyclical constancy in Judaism that keeps us grounded in current and fluid time. We celebrate the harvest, the trees, seasons of planting and cultivation. Our life cycle events mark transitions and growth in our lives- baby naming, bris, Bar/Bat Mitzvah, weddings. We also revere our ancestors and the past with the concept of L'Dor V'dor (from generation to generation). As Jews, we love to celebrate and we celebrate life in ways that are filled with hope and anticipation of the future.

The poems in this book have been written over a period of many years. Some have been part of services at Congregation Adat Reyim in Springfield, Va. Friends, family and several congregations use the poems as supplements to services, at home celebrations like Passover or Chanukah or read a poem at a Bris, wedding or baby naming. Some poems are part of collaborations with artists. Please feel free to use these poems at your celebrations, holidays, and synagogue or just for inspiration.

My hope is that this book nurtures your spirit and helps you discover something new about yourself and something engaging about Judaism. The first section of the book has poems for Jewish holidays. The second section celebrates life cycle events- baby naming, Bar/Bat Mitzvah, adoption, weddings, and even conversion to Judaism. A section in the back that helps to describe each holiday.

I hope you use these poems at your seder, Bar and Bat Mitzvahs, during synagogue services, a wedding or just for inspiration before a holiday or just pick up the book to reflect on an upcoming holiday.

May your days be filled with poetic inspirations and may some of those be found in this book.

-Sherri Waas Shunfenthal

Note to Readers

So much of Judaism helps us find our place in the world, connects us to one another or gives us reason to celebrate life. This book grew out of love for Judaism and a desire to share my view of the way Judaism connects us to the world. I've shared these poems with Jewish and non-Jewish friends who have found meaning in the poems. We have shared treasured discussions especially when they have found spiritual elements in the poems that relate to their own religion.

Here are some ways to use the poems in *Seasons of Prayer*.

Before a holiday, get into a contemplative mood by reading poems related to that holiday. Share a poem you like with your family. Have a discussion about the poem. Use some of the Chanukah, Passover or Shabbat poems at your home service.

Use a poem at a synagogue service. For instance you might add one of the Tashlich poems at your outdoor Tashlich service. If you like humor you might add the one about the ducks ("There will be a feast today at the lake for the ducks who will dine on Tashlich food – sinful bread tossed into the lake…"). Or you can add a poem to your synagogue bulletin for discussion.

If a friend or relative is getting married, you are welcome to read one of the wedding poems as a blessing or toast. There is a place to insert the name of your friend or relative in the poem.

Use one of the poems about Miriam or Esther in your sisterhood woman's service. Use Miriam poems at your seder and Esther poems at Purim.

When friends have had a non-Jewish family member coming to a Bar/Bat Mitzvah or wedding and want to give them a way to participate, they have borrowed a poem for that relative to read.

If there is an occasion when you are unable to get together with a loved one, send the book to them instead. If you find 'Prayerful Paradox' comforting, several people have included it with a condolence card.

Some of these poems were read at my woman's interfaith group. They are great opening for discussion or to share information about a Jewish holiday.

Please let me know how you have found new insights, comfort, or ways to utilize the poems in the book. I would love to hear from you.

Table of Contents

Torah: A Meditation   **1**

Selichot   **2**

For Giving   3
Selichot   4
Meditation on Forgiveness   5

Rosh Hashana   **6**

Anniversary of Creation   7
Teklah Gedolah – the Great Shofar Sounds   8
Creation   9
To Everything Turn, Turn   10

Tashlich   **11**

Begin Again   12
Let the Flow…   13
Tashlich   14

Yom Kippur   **15**

We Hunger, We Hope   16
Days of Awe (Yamin Nora'im)   17
Teshuvah   18
A Tone! Atone!   19
Blast of Strength   20
Every Year: Questions   21
The Shofar Sounds   22
Facing G-d   23

Sukkot   **25**

Stars at Sukkot   26
Open   27
Harvest   28

Simchat Torah   **29**

Waken the Words of Torah   30
L'Dor V'Dor   31
We Must Treasure Torah   32
With Torah   33
Torah, Our Tree of Life   34

Chanukah   **35**

Celebrating Freedom at Chanukah   35
Light in Darkness   37
Chanukah Wish   38
My Dreidel   39
Starry-eyed at Chanukah   40
Illumination   41
How Big Must the Miracle Be?   42
Dazzling   43

Tu B'Shevat   **44**

Let Me Be   45
What is the Sound of One Hand Clapping?   46
In the Garden   47
Sunflower Salutation   48

Purim   **49**

Esther Anointed   50
In the Palace   52
Celebrate, Esther   53
Esther, our Sister, Esther, our Queen   54

Passover   **56**

How is This Night Different From All Other Nights?   57
Remembering Our Stories at Passover   58
Women Dance!   60
After Bitter Herbs   61
Miriam's Faith   62
Miriam Knew   63

Spring Renewal   64
Together for Passover   65
Preparing for Passover   66
Passover Night (Poem for two voices)   67
Passover Night of Questions   68
Gathered Round the Passover Table   69

Yom HaShoah   **70**

Child of the Holocaust   71
Butterfly   72
Disappearing   73
A Woman Survivor of the Holocaust Speaks   74
    on Yom HaShoah
No Monument, no Memorial, no Prayer   75
Sedlcany Torah Speaks   77

Yom Ha'atzmaut   **80**

I Touch the Wall   81
Spaces of Time at the Wall   82

Shavuot   **83**

Shavuot   84
Torah   85
First Fruits   86
Honor, Love and Remember   87

Shabbat, Havdalah and Rosh Chodesh   **89**

The Flame of Shabbat   90
Prayer for Wholeness   91
Shabbat Light   92
Marriage Blessing for Shabbat   93
Shabbat   94
Havdalah   95
Rosh Chodesh, We Celebrate   96

Life cycle events **97**

    Wedding Blessing   98
    L'Dor V'Dor   99
    Entering the Covenant   100
    The Light in Your Eyes on Bat Mitzvah Day   101
    The Jewish People Gather   102
    Broken Glass Under the Chuppah   103
    Love Burning Brightly   104
    Adoption   105
    Chosen   106
    Welcome to Judaism   107
    Prayerful Paradox   108
    Remembering Loved Ones   109
    Yahrzeit   110
    Blessing Butterflies, Blessing Memories   111

Personal Reflections and Explanations **112**

Life Cycle Events **123**

Acknowledgments and Thank You **124**

    Shalom   127

About the Author **129**

Torah: A Meditation

Find a quiet spot
In that spot hear your heart
In your heart hear a prayer
In that prayer listen to your soul
In your soul discover Torah
In Torah seek wisdom
your people and your history
Feel the love of G-d
Surround you like a circle of light
Let the words of Torah
guide you...

To a quiet place inside your heart
In your heart you will hear a prayer
In your prayer you will find your soul
In your soul you will
feel the Love of G-d
surround you
like a circle of light
In the light discover Torah
In Torah
discover...

Selichot

שלום

We join together in blessing and with hope…

For Giving

Oh, G-d, help us to learn forgiveness.
Forgiveness is for give, not for get.

Forgiveness opens us mind and spirit.
Forgiveness is admitting we do not control everything.
Forgiveness is not giving in or giving up.
It is an act of strength allowing us to move forward
so we do not look behind in anger, resentment and pain.

May the sins we have committed be remembered
but not repeated. May we learn from our mistakes so we
can be closer to what is sacred in ourselves. May our judgments
of others be gentle in the coming year, our judgments of ourselves
be not harsh. Let us give from our hearts when we are wronged
or feel dishonored so that we are richer in spirit
and rise above transgressions that restrict us.

We are shattered vessels. Help us O G-d
to open to your divine love so that
together in the New Year we become whole.

Help us to forgive ourselves, our loved ones, our neighbors,
our acquaintances, our friends.
We are human. We are weak. We make mistakes.
O G-d bring us closer to what is sacred in ourselves
as we learn to reach for you. As we learn to seek and give
forgiveness, help us find faith to move forward this New Year.

Selichot
(a poem for two voices)

I shall
Return to G-d
in the morning when I wake.
Love G-d with my first breath
and all my soul.

      Return to G-d
      with all my heart, feeling G-d's loving presence
      with me through my day.

Return to G-d
with all my might, pay attention to the details of
G-d's magnificent creations and these words:
      Return to G-d
      I shall recite when I enter my house
      and when I leave so I remember and

Return to G-d
will be the light between my eyes
so I am guided to learn and follow all of G-d's commandments
and be holy unto my G-d.
      I shall praise G-d
      throughout my day and thank G-d for life
      when I lay down to sleep.

Blessing G-d when I wake
And remembering…

Meditation on Forgiveness

We join together in blessing and with hope
that G-d will hear our prayers, that our voices
will rise and fall like the tide into the flow of life where words
swim into a vastness larger than our individual selves.

Let us reach, deep down into the ocean
of our souls to a place where life moves more leisurely
less hectic than frantic everyday rushing.
A place where we can sway and dance and move
richly in time to the music of our soul. Let us
move like ocean seaweed rooted
but flowing easily with the currents, taking nourishment
from surrounding waters.

Let go of anger and frustrations that restrict us.
Reach inside, down to the depths to find
the current of forgiveness. Then flow easily forward. Forgive
ourselves, forgive others, forgive G-d.
Find Wholeness.

Rosh Hashana

Stardust and earth-dust merge with the Divine breath to create a single cell beginning life…

Anniversary of Creation

G-d's breath was and is the force
setting the world in motion
swirling, sweating, singing-
The world to be-
The world that is-
The world to come.

Melodic song, harmonic cycles-
birth/death, night/day, winter/spring,
awakening/sleeping, beginnings,
eternity.

G-d's breath calling the world
into being every moment
G-d's breath surrounding you.

Feel, hear G-d's breath
whispering in the winds, leaves swaying in breezes,
birdsong. Listen beyond
this moment now.

Breathe, open mind, open heart.
Be aware, alive with hope, without fear
surrounded by loving kindness all your days,
all your beginnings. Wholeness. Oneness. Amen.

Tekiah Gedolah- the Great Shofar Sounds.

There is the moment before the great shofar sounds.
Silence and anticipation. Waiting. Longing. I direct my faith
to the holiness of the sacred call. I pray. G-d listens.

Then the tone begins. One single note, One G-d.
The shofar blasting through my body. Tension as
the sound grows stronger and does not let go.
Words vanish. I ride the sound like a wave carrying me
to my truer self. I am open. Open to awareness. Paying full attention.
Open to belief and memory. Past and present merging. I am there
in the past and here now. Following the sound as if watching a bird
flying higher and higher into the distance until no longer seen.

As the sound of the great shofar ebbs away, I think, it sounds like life-
beginning in all its strength and glory then slowly ebbing
away into silence.

The sound lingers within me. I continue feeling
fully embraced. And so I believe G-d embraces us
in silence and in words, there and here
in death and in life.

Creation

Was it whispered?
shouted? musical or lyrical?
Was it a roaring big bang
or silent with no life yet to hear it?

Contraction into darkness. Expansion.
Infinite breath pouring forth pure energy.
Worlds bursting into being. Breath
shaping substance and matter into earth and sky,
wet and dry, earthly greens with swarming creatures
dark and light, day and night.

And when there was no companion, no partner, no witness
stardust and earth-dust merged with the Divine breath
to create a single cell beginning life.

Humans born. Awakening. In Eden.
Words and thoughts also born. Discovery and
re-discovery. Ongoing dynamic. Creation
shaped with words.

To Everything Turn, Turn

Season of anticipation-
green leaves changing to gold, orange,
red deep like wine
kaleidoscope of life turning, returning
under heaven, under sky. For every purpose
a circle harmonious.

Every year, Torah read from dawn
of Creation to this day. Beginnings
Reflections.

Time to look inward, examine our lives.
Turn. Turn to one another.
Ask forgiveness, ask for help.

Turn, turn to G-d for guidance.
Seek wisdom through prayer.

Turn, return with hope, faith and confidence.
Become our best vision of ourselves.
Begin.

Tashlich

Look into the water to find the reflection
of who you hope to be as time begins again this New Year.

Begin Again

Cast away sorrows and sins
Toss them into rivers-

Watch bubbles float upwards as
fresh dreams swell to the surface-

Sit quietly. Reflect
upon your tomorrows-

Rise-
Born anew.

Let the Flow...

Toss anger.
      Toss guilt.
            Toss sins

into the air where the breeze will reach
and hold them until they fall and
disappear into the waters.

Let the flow of water
carry hurtful thoughts downstream, away.
Let go until the soul is cleansed.

Forgive each other.
Forgive G-d.
Forgive yourself.

Look into the water to find the reflection
of who you hope to be as time begins
again this New Year. Reach inside.
Discover heart and soul
hopes and dreams that may have been forgotten.

Reach to find each other, share joys and sorrows
as time begins again this New Year.
Reach to find G-d in the open light of day,
by the land, by the waters.

Toss away fears as time begins again.
This New Year. Reach.

Tashlich

All our actions have an effect on the world..... or
one man's sin is some dumb duck's luck.

Temple notice:
There will be a feast today at the lake for the ducks who will dine on
creme de la Tashlich – sinful bread tossed into the lake.

First course:
sin a la self-indulgence
watch as ducks overeat, get too fat
waddle to and fro in discomfort.

Next course:
sin a la temper tantrum
watch as ducks squabble, shove each other,
fight for food, make loud quaking noises.

The ensuing course:
sin a la greed
watch as ducks push their own children
out of the way to vie for dry bread morsels.

Next:
sin a la envy
watch as one duck thinks "I want more, I'll get more"
"I'm worth more" but end up with a larger duck belly-ache.

The dessert:
sin a la arrogance
some ducks have over-bearing pride
but they are just like every other duck.

Ducks, appreciate what you have!
A good view, enough food, plenty of water,
the company of other fine ducks, enough to eat.
And do not worry-
Even though you have been fattened up-
no one is having Roast Duck for dinner tonight!

Yom Kippur

A tone! A single tone commands us, "Wake up! Wake up!"

We Hunger, We Hope

We hunger. We hope.
We reach. We pray.

Our need is great.
We enter into prayer hungry. Our prayers rise up
to force open the skies hoping you, O G-d will
hear our prayers and join with us.

We hunger. We thirst for G-d.
We hunger. We thirst for understanding.
We hunger. We thirst for guidance.

O G-d, we are empty. Fill us. Fill us and sustain us
with your loving kindness for the coming year.
May we be worthy of your love, O G-d
and find precious each day of the New Year.
May we find favor in your eyes, O G-d and
may your light shine upon us.

Help us, O G-d to notice the miracles of
daily existence. Let us thank you and reach for you
not only when we are hungry or thirsty
but when we are full of your blessings.   Amen.

Days of Awe (Yamin Nora'im)

The lawn is lit with fireflies darting through air like tiny acrobats
spinning and swooping.   I reach out, grab and cup one in my hand
opening my fingers just enough to see the luminescence I hold-

Suddenly transported back in time, I am seven years old
trembling with anticipation, catching a firefly, holding light
within my hand, feeling awe for this creature
seeking to be free, tickling my skin, fluttering about
using its light to seek its way home. Then letting go
watching the firefly dance away into the dark unknown
filled with tiny flying lamps illuminating the night like starlight.

Feeling part of the universe's vibrant vastness, being seven
when heaven was holding fireflies
I long to go back reaching to behold wonder.

Oh G-d, let me remember to behold your wonders
shift away from fears, possessions. Help me
look inside to shine my own light into the dark
 and always feel the miracle of life.
Remind me to awaken each morning to
days of awe.

Teshuvah

Like a Sabbath bride seeking my beloved
after wandering too far from home
longing to return...

The gates are wide open: Welcome
No reason to fear: Return

Seeking the path G-d has set before me.
Forgiving misdeeds, missteps, wrongdoings.
Leaving behind jealousies, regrets, resentment.
Eager to return to the best vision of myself...

The gates are wide open: Welcome
No reason to fear: Return

Acting mindfully with confidence. Determined
to be better, stronger, wiser yet acknowledging my
own human frailty. Knowing acts of tefillah, tzedakah
and teshuvah will help me find my path.....

The gates are wide open: Welcome
No reason to fear: Return

Yearning for closeness. Memory of oneness
desirous of fulfillment, awe and completion.
Seeking, searching...

The gates are wide open: Welcome
No reason to fear: Return
Live with great joy and blessedness
resolving never to stray too far again...

The gates are wide open: Welcome
No reason to fear: Return

A Tone! Atone!

The shofar pierces the heavens.
A tone! A single tone commands us,
"Wake up! Wake up!"

The singleness of the shofar's note
reflects our universal oneness.
The heavens spread wide
open for our collective cry to G-d.

Together in synagogue we seek forgiveness
for sins against ourselves, sins against family,
sins against friends, sins against our community,
sins against our planet,
sins against humanity, sins against G-d.

We plead with G-d to enter us in the Book of Life
for another year.
We hope to be better, stronger, wiser,
to take time to feel wonder and thanks everywhere we turn.
Wake up, wake up!

We pray for a good year, a year of harmony, health and peace-
a Year of At One-ment with ourselves, our
Jewish community, our faith
and our G-d.

Blast of Strength

The shofar lures me
into the power of its sound.
It strengthens me with its call
to Wake Up!
        Wake Up!
My soul feels thanks for this
blast of strength. I listen in awe.
Waves of emotion go through me
seeping into my blood so that
I think of all the new things
I want to do every year of my Life.

-David Mark Shunfenthal © 1999 (age 10)

Every Year: Questions

Unstructured days of summer make it hard to concentrate.
Then suddenly, days slip away into September.
With a gigantic sigh, school starts, weather changes,
so many things incomplete, unfinished. Promises to myself
remain unfulfilled and the Days of Awe arrive too soon.

Rosh Hashana grows closer to Yom Kippur. The holiness
of the days create a longing to cleanse my soul,
ask forgiveness, atone!

By the time I begin my Yom Kippur Fast, I am questioning:
Will this be the year I become my best self?
Will I accomplish what I set out to do? Will I allow fear to stop me?
Will I accept challenges with faith? Will I truly appreciate all I have?
Will I reach out to others in need? Will I go beyond complacency?
Will I find strength when I need it?
Will I strive to have greater compassion?

I pray fervently to be written in the Book of Life-
to have courage, to be better, stronger, wiser.
After the fast, together, we feast.
Our celebration of hope.

The Shofar Sounds

The shofar sounds-
Calling to Jewish people everywhere
to gather together families and friends.

The shofar sounds-
Piercing the air like a cry. Stirring collective memories.
Awakening an ancient past.

The shofar sounds-
Declares and punctuates. Drawing us together.
Compelling us to listen and recall.

The shofar sounds-
A symbol of rescue. When Abraham was willing
to sacrifice his son, the ram was sacrificed instead.

The shofar sounds-
Embraces us with spirited musical words
that resound and echo through our souls.
Tekiah, Teruah, Tekiah!

The shofar sounds-
An awesome cry. An ancient call.
Reaches over us, around us, beyond.
Calling simultaneously to us and to G-d.

Gathered in its grasp, we hope our prayers
are as strong, confident and far reaching
as the shofar sounds.

Facing G-d

Fasting brings us to a place where
we are neither rich or poor, educated or uneducated
owners of large homes or small
short in stature or tall.

We are all hungry, facing G-d together.
Hungry for G-d's forgiveness. We stand alone
but together- not in our finery
but with only the coat of our own making.

Time to examine the fabric of our lives.
We are the tailors. We have woven the cloth.
We have chosen the fabric. We have connected the threads.
We have added the buttons. We have made our coats to wear
each day before God.

We examine each thread, cast off the old
carefully inspecting for tears or unraveling.
What should be cast off? What should be remade?
What is acceptable in your eyes, O G-d?

We bow our heads in reverence thinking,
"Is my coat good enough? I vow to
restitch, reweave, recreate my coat in the New Year."

Some see threads unraveling and call for help,
"Please God help me to reweave my fabric. I had not noticed
how torn and frayed it is. Please help me connect the threads."

Others stand before G-d strutting peacock coats
Thinking, "Look at me, look at all I have achieved."
But a peacock is just a bird with pretty feathers.
"Please God, let there be meaning in these colors
as I come before you."

Still others find their suit is comfortable. It is not too big
too small or disheveled. "Please G-d let me wear
my coat with dignity another year."

Individually and together we stand before G-d
in the suits of our own making. Collectively in spirit
We become One as together we ask forgiveness.

"O G-d, Humble us before you. We vow to try to be better people.
Please inscribe us in the Book of Life for another year."

Sukkot

Look through the open spaces, see infinity…

Stars at Sukkot

All shelters temporary.
Ground beneath us always shifting so
Look up, look up
into the heavens. Gaze upon the stars
when unsure of where you are
or where you are meant to be.

Look up, look up!
The stars are above us guiding us.
Same stars our ancestors gazed upon
to navigate the lonely spaces
wandering through the desert, working
and harvesting the fields, building new structures.

Look up, look up!
Stars like grains of sand in the desert, infinite and
more numerous than can be imagined. All is
temporary. Walls too easily can crumble into dust and mud.

Look up, look up!
We are stardust, creating our narratives
for the next generation. Invite friends, family,
neighbors to come together under the stars.
Eat inside the sukkah, share food, share stories.
Keep this special time in your heart, outdoors, under sky.
G-d's canopy of peace spread over you.
Look up, look up!

Open

Abraham and Sarah's Tent
always open on all sides- north, south, east and west
because Abraham and Sarah were open
had nothing to hide.

Open
for strangers who might come needing shelter
from desert heat, for travelers and neighbors
to enter and receive blessings,
conversation, food, comfort and wine.

Open
to see dawn's radiant glow
with sky above and earth below
and G-d all around.

Open
knowing all dwellings are temporary
but should be built with strength and simplicity.
Look through the open spaces, see infinity.
Life is fragile, so be open and unafraid.

May your days and Sukkah be
open like Abraham and Sarah's tent
filled with love, family, friends.
Peace Fullness.
Open.

Harvest

The vibrant colors of autumn awaken us
as we reach inside ourselves
to explore the colors of our lives.

We celebrate the majesty
fullness, ripeness of the season and ourselves
full of possibilities, willing to take chances
risk new beginnings.

We gather in the fruits of our labors
the bounty of our harvest and praise
our creator for this magnificent season.

We gather in families and friends
looking back on hours well spent together.
We know the glorious colors of autumn are short-lived.
We gather in good memories to help face the bareness of winter
and draw on harvest memories.

Relax, reflect, pray for the coming New Year:
May it be a good year
a year of peace, a year of hope
with a harvest that is bountiful.
There is hard work ahead.

Simchat Torah

Mystical meaning of our stories, our heritage, our faith unfolding...

Waken the Words of Torah

Ancient words carefully scribed
letter by letter upon parchment of Torah.
Words silent, resting
waiting for the voice to breathe them into being.

Awaken the ancient words of Torah. Waken us
to listen. Blow the breath of life upon the parchment
make the words dance
to ageless rhythms and chants.

Let the mystical meaning of our stories, our heritage
our faith unfold. Come to the words in partnership
with intention and attention-
Make what is visible to the eye
audible to the ear, the heart and the soul.

Awaken words of Torah as we
follow our story into the past
and make it our future.

Breath blows the seeds of Judaism to create life.
Let Torah be strengthened each time we speak
with our hearts, our souls, the force of our being.

L'Dor V'Dor-

Generation to Generation
(A thank you to our Rabbis, Educators, Parents)

Torah began long before the first scrolls were written.
Genesis of Torah was with our teachers-
Abraham, Isaac, Jacob, Sarah, Rebecca, Rachel and Leah
who carried faith in their hearts, wisdom in adherence to belief.

When Moses climbed Mt. Sinai, he carried the words whispered
to his ancestors on the wings of G-d's breath. He descended Sinai
with G-d's words, a code of conduct- our way of life.
On the passage to the Promised Land
Torah was shaped with stories of our people, our journeys
scribed and described generation to generation.

Torah became our contract with G-d to remember
our people, share our stories, teach our children,
and learn from the past.

Teachers and sages through the ages have
set us upon a path of learning rich in discovery of Torah's meaning.

Teachers, rabbis, parents and families
are our keepers of traditions, interpreters of our stories
guiding our way of life, feeding us from the Jewish family tree
helping us to thrive and survive generation to generation.

We Must Treasure Torah
(a responsive reading)

Reader:
When G-d gave us the Torah, there was thunder and lightning
and the great call of the shofar beckoning us to Torah's wisdom.

Congregation:
Torah is a tool to help us build our lives.
Torah makes us part of a greater truth.
Torah's lessons give us light.

Reader:
Torah's truths lead us to discovery. If we get lost
Torah helps us find the way. If we are in darkness
Torah awakens us to the dawn. If we are weak
and seek Torah's wisdom, we gain strength.

Congregation:
We must treasure Torah. Hold the force of the words
deep inside where the spirit of life is eternal.

Congregation:
Torah is G-d's gift to us. We must give this gift to our children
and our children's children. Torah is part of us.
We are part of Torah past, present, and future.

With Torah

With Torah
Our souls become unburdened-
Our spirits are renewed-
Our thoughts take wings-
Our lives become whole-

We are part of one family
following the guidance of Torah
yesterday, today and
through eternity.

Torah, Our Tree of Life

(In honor of our Torah Teachers)

A seed is patted firmly into the ground with hands and heart.
Teachers of Torah create life with the seed they plant
deep within our soul. Each seed nourished with devotion
to learning and discovery. The seed bursts open and grows
as we students care for it with love, learning and knowledge.

The sun warmly shines on our seed as our teachers
shed their brilliance upon us. The seed sprouts into a tree
growing stronger and sturdier as we students
strive to study and learn.

Tree roots grow deeper. Branches increase their number
as students, teachers and friends nurture
our interest and desire to know Torah.

The tree bears fruit feeding and sustaining the Jewish people as we
reflect upon and live Torah's teachings.
Students become teachers in a circle of magic
passing our knowledge from generation to generation so
 the Jewish people can continue to climb it, cling to it, celebrate it-
Torah, our Tree of Life.

Chanukah

Whirl, twirl. Have faith, take a chance.

Celebrating Freedom at Chanukah

We gather together on Chanukah
to recount the ancient story of
strength, hope, freedom and light
as we remember the Maccabees
who fought with all their might
for what they believed to be right-
freedom for the Jewish people.

Our memory of the Maccabees reminds us
that a small group of people can make a
large difference in the world.
We recall the miracle of the oil lasting for eight days.
We have faith miracles are possible.

We join together to cherish our freedom
and freedom for all people.
We know that we must always fight for
the right to live what we believe.
We pray for strength, hope, freedom and light-
the spirit of this Chanukah night.

Light in Darkness

Dark of winter we remember
we are shattered vessels.

Too easy to lose our way. Too frightened
too cold, too much sorrow in the world.
Where can we find victory over darkness?

Each night when we light the menorah
we light our way. Light one by one
candle. Build brightness
slowly.

At sundown, join in the miracle of creation
rekindling the lights each night
until the whole menorah is ablaze.
Flames dancing, pure spirit rising
Reaching, reminding us-
Be patient, have faith,
cultivate fortitude.

Miracles shine through darkness.

Chanukah Wish

This is my Chanukah wish-

To kindle holy lights
so that at nightfall the world is lit with hope and wisdom
to fight against hatred, greed and despair.
May the light be spread among the nations
and be as widespread as the twinkling of stars shining.
May the light illuminate a path of love, goodness and generosity.
May it be like the menorah - strength to strength, candle to candle
brightening until the glow that warms our homes and hearts
warms the hearts of women, men and children everywhere.

May we rededicate ourselves to faith, peace and justice
with every candle that is lit each Chanukah night!

My Dreidel

4 sided body, lonely stem on its head. I hold it
between my fingers then swiftly spin my dreidel round and round.
Momentum driven by desire for a favored result. Get ready.
Spin, dreidel, spin!

Who is the master spinner? Who decides when dreidel drops?
What will be my fate, luck, destiny? Will I know
if I don't take a risk? Let the game begin.
Spin, dreidel, spin!

Nervous anticipation. On which side will dreidel fall?
Nun: Receive nothing but wait! I can try again.
Gimel: Receive a miracle, gather all possibilities to me.
Hay: Receive half, which holds promise.
Shin: Give back, one must never keep it all.
Spin, dreidel, spin!

Play the game over and over. Take your turn.
For what do you yearn? Begin.
Spin dreidel spin!

Nun: Can you create something from nothing?
Gimel: Feel blessed, have it all.
Hay: Hope! You are halfway there.
Shin: Return- it is all yours, only temporarily.

Whirl, twirl. Have faith. Take a chance. Dance, dreidel, dance!
Turning, yearning, returning. Every time you fall, rise once more!
Every time you rise, celebrate!
Spin, dreidel, spin!

Starry-eyed at Chanukah

Stars in their infinite glory thrill the dark night of sky
dazzling us like a million jewels.
I marvel at the wonder, miracle and mystery.

Winter is here. In the darkness of night
within our homes we create our own miracle of lights.

We order the universe of light to increase
brightness each night in our menorahs.
It never fails to excite - whole sky of stars
shining, sparkling, shimmering in my menorah.

Delicious, cozy, warm, happy Chanukah!

Illumination

Our spirits were dark.
Then the walls of the temple were wondrously illuminated
by one small dancing flame. Enough oil!
Beginning of celebration. Triumph of freedom over oppression.
Radiance reigning over darkness. Responsibility to
re-build and restore. Slowly. The light growing
brighter, shining from within
and onto the walls of the Temple.

Every Chanukah night we remember.
Add one more candle to the menorah.
Add one more mitzvah. Watch miracles grow brighter-

Eight nights to celebrate and the shammas to light:
The miracle of faith.
The miracle of strength of spirit.
The miracle of hope and promise.
The miracle of freedom.
The miracle of religious choice.
The miracle of freedom to speak and live without fear.
The miracle of having enough.
The miracle of being together to share.

These miracles acknowledge our
obligation to Tikkun Olam.-
illumination and repair of the world.

Place your menorah in the window for all to see-
Jewish spirit dancing, flames dancing, hope dancing!
Freedom... everlasting light and life.

How Big Must the Miracle Be?

A small vessel of oil, that's all.
To keep the flame alive
for eight days and eight nights.

Miracles arrive in small and large ways,
a surprise. A chance meeting, a flask of oil,
an unexpected package an offer of help,
not being hurt when in an accident,
a butterfly adding color to a dreary day,
the doctor calling to say everything is okay.

How big does the miracle have to be?

Is it the sudden smile on a child's face when (s)he spins a dreidel?
Is it the anticipation as we light the next candle?
Is it being in the presence of family and friends?
Is it the flame itself? Or the fire within?
Is it watching and feeling the candles flicker and dance?

There is always a chance to enrich our lives, be a blessing to all.
The biggest miracle of all is being able to kindle the flame
become the spark creating a fire- desire to love life,
be together, help others.

A small vessel of oil, that's all.
How big does the miracle have to be?

Dazzling

Eight Chanukah nights
a wonderful story of victory and glory
miracles we re-live and share
every year-

The first night- we kindle one light, begin.
Second night- two lights, a grin.
Next night, three-
Dazzling as can be!
Four, I adore the dancing flames.
Five, look how they come alive.
Six, there are no tricks.
Seven, just the glorious heaven
of leaping, rising flames growing brighter each night.
Eight sparkling lights like a thousand jewels,
a thousand hopes, a world of dreams.

Tu B'Shevat

Reach upwards toward dreams, grow sturdier, stronger, bud and blossom…..

Let Me Be...

Let me be like the tree-
Hibernate, peel off layers
get to the bare essentials, find
depths in the gray silence of winter.

Let the world swirl around me.
Let the snow fall. Let me warm myself
by sinking inside my roots, seeping
and searching within myself for nourishment.

Let me be like the tree. I too need time
to rest, rejuvenate, and replenish my spirit
find moments of deep solitude within myself
so that in spring
I can reach upward toward sky
reach toward dreams
be ready to grow sturdier, stronger
bud and blossom
ready to embrace any raging winds.

What is the Sound of One Hand Clapping?

I took a writing and meditation workshop.
The professor had us concentrate on the ancient koan:
What is the sound of one hand clapping?
The question haunted me.
Until yesterday.

Sitting in the park, I gazed upward.
Golden tinged leaves at the end of
the highest tree branch were flittering,
fluttering, furiously waving like
banners proclaiming magnificence
of turquoise, sun filled sky. Symphony
of leaf song reaching, dancing,
celebrating almost -autumn. Clapping
in anticipation, joy. I heard them.
When I looked up.

Definition: koan- a paradoxical anecdote or a riddle that has no solution.

In the Garden

Life springing forth.
Roots grabbing hold.
Stems of strength reaching upward.
Buds ready to blossom.
Flowers soaking in sunlight beginning
to open their colorful blossoms.
Fruits, herbs and vegetables ripening
under the gardener's nurturing care.

Slow process of growth
reminds us to be patient.
Slow down, soak in the sun.
Let troubles vanish, let thoughts flow
easily like gentle streams over pebbles.

Take a breath.
Time is eternity, here
in the garden where
Eden is found.

Sunflower Salutation

I offered you water
plowed the land so you could grow
day and night I watched over you
waiting to know- Will you flourish?
Will you be rich in color and
offer your dazzling beauty to the world?

Now you are here, golden radiance and grace
swaying on your stems in sunflower fields.

I admire, am inspired by golden blooms of grace.
I walk in silent worship, in awe beyond words, beyond space.

Filled with sun song, I suddenly long to take a flower by the stem-
sway with me, dance with me, golden bloom of sunshine, dance!

I offer you to friends, to lovers, to the world.
Shining forth. From earth created to the earth return
your shining seeds forever more.

O Fill us, flowers of the sun
with smiles, with joy, with love.
Sunflowers, Dance!

Purim

Identity hidden. Beauty revealed.

Esther Anointed

Esther 2:12 "...according to the regulations for the women, for thus were the days of their preparation apportioned: six months with oil of myrrh, and six months with perfumes and preparations for beautifying women."

Esther, orphan and exile. So young, yet chosen to enter the palace. Anointed with oil of myrrh, bathed in perfumes, pampered. Chosen to begin a life so different from the one she knew.

Inside the palace, she gained favor with Hegai,
the eunuch who was enamored of her quiet dignity- no false pride.
Her restraint was not contrived.
Hegai gave her seven choice maidens
she treated with kindness. She had no wishes for riches
nor was she envious of other beauties.
She stood alone, her identity hidden.

Cleansed, perfumed and pampered, the eunuch persuaded her
to be herself, to become as polished as the palace gemstones-
mother-of-pearl, porphyry, crystal until she shone to perfection.

Esther's inner beauty and strength sparkled. Identity hidden
but beauty revealed.   The King wished to possess her perfection.
Nothing he offered could buy her love. She asked only for what
Hegai advised.

Her quietude was not meekness. Her truth was her dignity.
Simplicity and youth. The King came to love her.
She was like no other. Amidst extravagance and excess,
she never demanded and never refused. And when she was needed,
she was strong. She made no demands, she made requests.
She risked her life. She was brave. She made choices
that saved her people. For eternity remembered on Purim.

So when you celebrate Purim, remember, Respond with dignity,
make choices that are wise. Celebrate, for you do not know
when you may be chosen. If a child young as Esther could be chosen
you too may be chosen to lead, or save your people.

Celebrate- who knows if you are only one step away
from truth and discovering your strength
who you are or who you may become.
Be like Esther, the anointed one...

In the Palace

Esther is fasting. Esther is praying. Alone.
Hidden away. In the palace of the King.
Only able to see the King when summoned.
Isolated in the palace of the King. Only Uncle Mordechai knows
her true identity. Have her people forsaken her?
Has God forsaken them all? Who can change a royal decree?
Beauty is not enough. Courage alone is not enough.

Esther is fasting. Asking her people to join her in fast and prayer.
She is praying for strength. She is praying for her people.
She is praying for redemption.
Isolated in the palace of the King.
Praying. Fasting.
Hoping. Reaching.

Esther is reaching for G-d, asking G-d to be her partner.
Asking G-d to be her strength.
And so she approaches the King's throne
with G-d by her side. With her people in her prayers.
Esther is revealed. G-d is there.
In the palace. In the story.
In the prayer. In the hope.
We are saved!

Celebrate, Esther

Like a Persian river seeking to connect with sea
action flowing seamlessly round obstacles.
Story unfolding, not without risk.

Haman's lots have been cast.
Cast of characters chosen
yet it seems one presence, not mentioned
is missing from the story and yet...
Surely, the winding ease with which the tale develops
without disaster, with grace, with blessing
must mean, perhaps, a miracle...

Take a chance, dear Esther, take a chance on G-d
to restore your life and the life of your people.

Have faith, dear Esther
though you walk on the edge between life and death
choose, take a risk while knowing the lots are cast.

Within palace walls that constrict and confine, even there
you have choices, so lead from your heart and head.
Act with direction and purpose. Move with ease,
faith, bravery and hope. Believe
in the unseen that makes rivers flow
shaping paths for centuries.

Accept the miracle from wherever it comes then
Celebrate! Life!

Note: In Megillat Esther, (Scroll of Esther), G-d is not mentioned
unlike every other book in Torah. Megillat Esther actually means
"revealing the hidden."

Esther, our Sister. Esther, our Queen.

1.
Vashti, the Persian Queen would not undress, dance
or debase herself before the Persian King Ahashauerus
King of the party not the people.
Vashti tired of Ahashauerus' demands vehemently said "No!"
King Ahashuerus angered cast her aside like bad tasting oats
declaring, "I will find another Queen."

2.
"Esther, gentle Esther I have a plan," whispered Mordechai
to his niece.
"Go to the King. Let your beauty help you.
Then, someday you will convince the king to save our people."
"Mordechai, warrior uncle, I am not that brave. I too love our people
but how can my beauty save them?" Esther asked.
"Esther, gentle Esther, make your beauty speak first, then use your
words to the King. He is weak. Make your beauty speak."

Chosen from among throngs of beauties, Esther wore radiance
wrapped in pride. She excited the King with her beauty,
her youth, her gentle wit, her stories.
In Persia good stories are like narcotics- they hypnotize.
Esther told stories of people she loved, family,
ancient Jewish warriors.
She sang sweet praises to the King. He listened entranced
through a drunken, drugged revelry.

Esther was not seduced by Ahashauerus' lively party-going madness
celebrations. When she placed the crown upon her head
she became confident, articulate.
A queen poised and assured as if she had nothing to fear.

Beauty defined by dignity, Esther walked with grace.
She held her head high. When King Ahashuerus saw her bearing
dignity dressed in beauty,
it was something he wished to possess.
Ahasheuarus - powerless partyer, impotent king wished to possess
dignity, power and beauty. Beauty cannot be possessed.

Beauty alone cannot save you. Beauty did not save Vashti.

3.
Esther came to the palace to serve the King.
Esther was beauty defined by dignity.
Esther anticipated Ahashasuerus' every need
through his drug-eyed Persian-haze
he thought he saw her love and devotion.
In Esther's eyes was the love of her people, love of justice.
Ahasheuarus came to trust her.
He listened to her stories. He trusted her words.
He trusted her beauty. He thought he possessed it.
Beauty such as Esther's cannot be possessed.

Ahasheuarus trusted Esther's words clothed with dignity -
beauty dressed in confidence. Esther served him.

4.
She served the King the truth about Haman, whom the King trusted.
Esther made Ahasheurarus, the impotent King potent once more
by Hanging Haman. Haman of the three cornered hat
-the hat that hung on his head in this three-cornered tale.
Haman cornered by his own desire for power.
Mordechai, cornered Haman with warrior deceit.
Esther, cornered Haman with her words to Ahashuerus.
Haman, destroyed. His head hung in shame
in this three-cornered allegory.

5.
Purim, O Purim. Get mixed up. Drink a lot. Plan a plot.
Destroy. Deceive. Deny.
But believe -Esther was dignity defined.
And if you choose to accept this story
Or choose to think of it as allegory
Remember Esther was beauty clothed in dignity.

And if you get a bit confused, remember her story
of we Jews. Esther was dignity defined
Esther, our sister. Esther, our Queen.
Esther, a young girl saved us with her words.

Passover

Too busy with our lives, we might forget to remember our stories…

How is This Night Different from All Other Nights?

On all other nights
G-d looks down from the heavens and breathes a heavy sigh.
G-d sees gas guzzling, factory fumes
devastation of the land
idol worship of silver, gold, brass and name brands
people coveting other people's stuff
fighting, stealing, destruction and war
And G-d looks down and says, "Oy!"

But on Passover night
G-d looks down upon his people
sees them seated round the Passover table
talking, remembering and telling stories
and G-d breathes a satisfied sigh
and says "It is good!"

Remembering Our Stories at Passover

Too busy with our lives, we might forget
to remember our stories, become pages
without binding scattered in the wind.

So we gather on Passover to tell and retell our stories
of exodus to freedom. Seder helps us put thoughts in order.
We recant our beginnings so we know how far
we have traveled.

We tell of journeys: Wandering through the desert accepting
G-d's commandments, our covenant with our Creator.
We speak of Miriam and Moses who awakened
the Jewish people to escape enslavement and
have faith in G-d while crossing the desert.

We tell of desires, journeys to promised lands,
the voyages of our grandparents – like my own grandparents' parting
from family and friends at age 18
to cross the ocean in steerage on a ship.
They came with only 10 commandments,
each other's love, faith, hope
and the dream to discover America.

We remember children who perished in death camps.
Some who escaped. We tell of freedom fighters and
survivors who had the courage to rebuild their lives.

We pause to appreciate parents
who moved us to better neighborhoods
then established communities and synagogues so
we children could build a place of belonging.

We think about Sabras born in Israel because their parents
crossed the desert fighting for freedom, cultivating the earth
with sweat and dreams to nourish the land and
make it rich in milk, hope and honey.

Traditions. Transitions. Wanderings.
New lands. New languages. New cultures.
Our memories.   We gather year to year to tell and retell
our stories- the threads holding the binding
of our Jewish family book together.

Women Dance!

We, the women, packed with simplicity, eagerly,
but with fear of the unknown.
We baked bread hurriedly, holding children close while
singing sweet soothing songs. One luxury we packed:
our musical instruments
to express our longing for freedom, for G-d
the music of our hearts. Ready to cast out tyranny
risk everything for faith and freedom. Fleeing with
soldiers at our backs. Too easy to lose hope.

Suddenly sea walls miraculously split apart.
Travel quickly when G-d opens a pathway. Do not tarry
or all will be lost! Miriam urges us to move quickly through the
walls of water! Leave the past behind. Trust.
There is a new world across the Sea!

We, the women and children move as one
on shaky feet made stronger with each step of faith
moving closer to the promised land.

Safely on the shore, some of us collapse with relief
some sob, some falter, some shout with joy. Miriam rallies
us. She grabs her tambourine, begins to dance, singing praises
to G-d who opened the walls for us, our families, our people.
We, the women rise and join the dance of life.
Celebrate, the old is gone, the new is here.

Celebrate! Believe in our G-d who has liberated us,
led us out of slavery. Do not be afraid. But do not revel too long.
The work ahead is hard and not without need of G-d.
Move ahead with faith.

After Bitter Herbs

Maror, heavy and harsh like the bricks
made by slaves to build the Egyptian Temple.
Maror, bitter enough to bring tears to your eyes-
eaten with matzoh, the bread that does not rise.

A life cannot rise in slavery or
move forward in bitterness.
A heart cannot take flight where there is no hope.

So together, let us remember the past
while looking forward in faith. Help us
find light in taking the first step away
from bitterness and enslavement.

There are blessings in gratitude.
Jubilance in freedom.
Redemption in beginnings.

After bitter herbs, we feast.

Miriam's Faith

Miriam had no children but she gave birth
to infant Moses by the waters of Egypt safely
placing him in his womb like basket into the sea of Reeds.
Hiding in bulrushes, she watched her brother
float toward freedom and life.

Miriam summoned courage, spoke softly to laughing princesses
who quickly found him and became enamored. Miriam
courageously suggested a Hebrew woman, her mother
to feed and care for the baby who lived and breathed.
Soon birthed again as Moses.

Miriam, a prophetess, grew up believing Moses would lead
the liberation of her people. She brought Moses home when
he was needed to free his people from slavery. She followed Moses
across the Red Sea that opened like a woman's womb to give
birth to her people. Miriam the midwife
delivered the mothers of Israel safely
then sang to her newborn children, praises to G-d.

In the desert Miriam's well of faith nourished her people when
they were thirsty. Her song soothed the spirit. She
spoke of G-d, told stories of her children reborn into freedom.

Miriam knew that to grow we must move from slavery.
Look to the future. Awake. Rejoice. Dance.
Sing of being born. Anew.

Miriam Knew

Miriam knew
there would be a reason to celebrate
And brought along her timbrel
Miriam who
Had faith when she put her baby brother Moses in a basket
made of reeds and watched him float away
Miriam knew
he would return safely someday
to lead the Jewish people away from slavery
Miriam knew
wth faith you can move forward
Miriam knew
It is not easy to be a Jew
Miriam knew
Music and dance unite us
Miriam knew
How to give comfort and hope
Miriam knew
That wandering in the desert just means
one foot in front of the other and manna will appear
if you believe; she had no fear
Miriam
sister, friend, adviser
lover of song, of dance, of life
Miriam knew

Spring Renewal

Emboldened by the purple, white and yellow crocuses
whose blossoms fill me with awe so soon after the last
winter snowfall, I feel optimistic, ready to press through dirt
to clean and put my home in order. Longer
sunlit days make me feel ready to break through the
narrow places in my life, move away from enslavement of
old habits and patterns that have become
vows broken since Rosh Hashana.

Passover is a time of renewal. I examine where I have been
what pulls me back, what sets me free. Like the Israelites
on the passage to the Promised Land
I hope to cross with faith into the future.
Be ready to begin.

Oh G-d help me move away from what binds me. Help me
move into the future with hope and strength. Help me
to honor my people with faith in my G-d . Give me
strength to take the first steps towards rejuvenation.
Let me be thankful for what I have not what I want.
Awaken my appreciation of simple things like
colorful crocuses rising up through snow.

Together for Passover

Wandering in the desert far from the comfort zone of home
unsure of where we were going, fearful.
Would we stumble and fall, not be able to rise?
Terrified of moving forward in the swirling
raging waters of the unknown, praying
for G-d to bring us to far shores
safely across the Red Sea.

Tonight we
pass the matzoh
pass the salt water tears
pass the charoset
pass the bitter herbs
pass the wine
Cross the sea of memory-
recall life's curses, struggles and many blessings.
Reflect upon distances traveled, we remember
ancestors who built and labored, loved and longed
for more so that are together
safe in this moment.

We pray for G-d to grant us strength
grant us peace, grant us good journeys
to cross raging seas safely. Open the way for us to
see clearly to the other side. And may we be together
next year to share our stories, share our food,
share our love, our lives.

Preparing for Passover
(in memory of my mom)

Preparing for Passover
busy stirring matzoh meal, eggs, oil and spices
putting my hands deep into batter
gathering sticky dough between my palms
pressing and shaping slowly, round
matzoh balls perfectly shaped…

The phone rings. My hands are thick with matzoh ball
doughiness. I dry off my hands, wishing it was mom calling to
ask how my matzoh balls are shaping up. Then we'd laugh
as she'd ask- hard or soft? Then she would recall
her mom's fluffy, soft matzoh balls and tell and how she
learned to make hard ones just for Dad then send
soupy kisses through the phone to add flavor.

I wish you were here, mom. I wish you could join us for dinner.
Most of all I wish you were standing here beside me
talking to me as we cooked. I drop matzoh balls
into the soup one by one letting my tears add saltiness.
Three years since you are gone.

Making charoset, I chop walnuts remembering
how we laughed as we banged walnuts with a mallet
against the cutting board. Making grunting noises for fun
as if we were engaged in such hard work.
I add this this sweet memory to my recipe.

Passover is a time of memory-
sorrows and joys come to our table. Remember.

Passover Night
(Poem for two voices)

We come together
we come together to remember

      To remember those who enslaved us
      enslaved us and would not let us go

Let us go when we would not let go
not let go of the dream of freedom
      The dream of freedom we remember
      we remember and safeguard and cherish

Cherish the promise of a place
that lay beyond the shackles
      The shackles that bind and destroy the spirit
      the spirit ever searching, seeking

Seeking to travel beyond vast desert emptiness
Desert emptiness, hungering to be filled
      Filled with fear or filled with faith? We chose
      Chose faith that followed us during forty years

Forty years wandering in the desert
in the desert hoping, praying to finally enter
      The Promised Land
      Filled with strength, hope, faith and freedom--
      Our Promised Land.

Passover Night of Questions

It is why we are here
together
every year at Passover
to ask questions:
to ask who
to ask when
to ask why
to ask how

We are here
connected by questions

living within the questions
thriving in our quest
for learning and knowing
past, present, future

forming a bond by asking-
and sharing in the responses
creating our narratives
we exchange thoughts, anecdotes, stories
we listen. we pray and give thanks.
our questions are our path to freedom
opening us to possibilities and hope.

So we join together asking
who, asking how, asking why, when and where,
here, now together learning, loving, laughing, eating and
celebrating freedom.

Gathered Round the Passover Table

Gathered round the Passover table
fragrant scents of charoset stir us to desire dreams
while remembering the crossing of the Red Sea
turbulent and raging but open and ready
for us to cross to safety.

We recite together the story of leaving bondage-
the taste of freedom sweet- sweet like desserts
and family togetherness. Wine, prayer, stories and dinner
make us dizzy with fullness. The fullness of friends and
family. Ancestors join us
as we share memories, remembering
makes the past, present.
Laughter and conversation
echo through time with celebration.
We are free, we are Jewish,
here, now, together.
Let us be thankful for our blessings.
Let us be healthy and strong.
Let us be together
again next year.

Yom HaShoah

My hope us one bright yellow star shining over my heart.

Child of the Holocaust

I reach
grasp at life
huddle near friends
in this camp of death.

Shallow breath.
Wounds so deep
I fear I may disappear.

Darkness looms near.
Hope is holy.
My hope is one bright
yellow star shining
over my heart.

Butterfly

Black ashes
rise into
Sky.

Butterfly
desperately tries
to escape into
Blue.

Black smoke looms
dark above. Destroys.

Lives too quickly
ended. Butterfly
fly away from this
dark night of day.

Disappearing

Stripes of black
like anger flash across
emaciated body
disappearing into white
clothing covering bone and flesh.

Heart underneath has not turned to stone.
Heart beats life and love, pain
and yearning to be free.

Pain disappears in death.
Love lingers on.
Freedom.

A Woman Survivor of the Holocaust Speaks
on Yom Hashoah-
Holocaust Remembrance Day 1993

"There is not a language, a dictionary of words
to describe the horror," she said. I try to shut
out images forming in my mind from the words she speaks.
She must shut out her memories.

I want to run, repulsed at images she creates in my mind.
I can only learn lessons of the past by listening,
learning from one who was there and saw
felt, and survived.

I hear the weeping, crying, screaming voices of
children calling "Momma! Poppa!" I feel the
reaching cries to G-d
"Where are you?"

I am touched when she tells of the heroism of those who
helped each other by sharing food, doing each other's work
when one was too tired, encouraging each other to try, please
to stay alive.

I hear how those that were starving gave her extra food
because she was so young
so very young.

She tells us to remember.
She tells us that in remembering, there is hope
for the future.

No Monument, no Memorial, no Prayer[1]

There is no monument, memorial, or prayer
that can erase the anguish of those who lived through the terror
and torture of tyrants and common people
so filled with hate.

There is no monument, memorial, or prayer
that can bring back the lives of
the One, Two, Three, Four, Five, Six Million
Women, Men, Boys, Girls and Infants
whose innocent lives were brutally taken.

There is no monument, memorial, or prayer
that can silence the moan that rises from our hearts
when we recall those who perished.

There is no monument, memorial, or prayer
that gives adequate expression to the pain that is deeper
than our gentle souls can bear to remember

Yet we do not seek revenge for the past.
What our enemies sought to destroy
we seek to strengthen and sanctify
in devotion to the lost.

As we dedicate our Torah, we rededicate ourselves
to the sanctity of all life and the continuing
history of all Jewish people.

Whatever evil comes upon our earth
we will do our best not to let G-d's words be destroyed
by hatred or apathy.

---

[1] (written July 1995 for the Holocaust restored by scribes for Adat Reyim)

We restore our Torah. We restore a life
The life of the Torah is the life of our people.

Our Torah binds us to G-d and to every Jewish person
past, present and future yesterday, today and eternity.

Sedlcany Torah Speaks

The Sedlcany Torah was rescued from Sedlcany, Czechoslavakia and
restored by Congregation Adat Reyim in Springfield, Virginia. It was
restored rather than just displayed. Congregation Adat Reyim currently
uses this Torah. This poem is in the voice of that Torah. In Judaism, a
Torah is never destroyed, it is buried. As long as it is used, it lives. The
Sedlacany Torah speaks...

Survivor

Wizened, wise. Huddled, hunched unto myself.
Horrors mark my 200 year old soul. Horrors no life can imagine.
I have witnessed death, destruction, terror, pain.
Handled with hatred. I became a number
without identity, without a name.
Desecrated, defiled, I grew diminished. Exposed to fire,
water, and air, I became brittle, dry, shrunk and shriveled.
Life inside death, death inside life.

Memory

Long ago I remember that I lived in the arks of my Jewish families.
I was warm, protected, clothed in majesty.
I felt cherished. Proud. Lifted by my people, their voices, their love.
I felt their energy coursing through my words awakening life as
my words were recited, read aloud.
I remember, my Jewish people.

Silence

Silence entered me -
the silence of no voices reaching for my words.
I was imprisoned in silence. Imprisoned in fear.

Words

And yet, hidden deep inside some secret cavern of myself
beyond the disbelief was a hint of hope
that willed me to survive. I huddled
over the words that were once my life. Terrified that the
words might be lost forever in the void of darkness and despair.
I slumped over the words with my last ounce of energy
trying to protect G-d's words. Even when my soul cried,
"Where is G-d?" I knew G-d in the words.

Hope and Rescue

I know the darkness of the void.
I know how easily people and words can be
lost forever. Only with hope was I suspended
between all my yesterdays and tomorrows, shadow and light.

Hope once a dream, becomes reality!
My words are restored (by Congregation Adat Reyim).
I am rescued, wakened from non-being.

I am the Torah. I am witness.
I am restored. I remember.

The Womb

In my new synagogue, in my ark, I curl into myself,
safe, inside my Jewish womb safe, yet still I tremble.
I need to feel your heartbeat. I need to hear your voices.
I need to feel your strong, protective arms. Cradle me like a baby.
Carry me through the congregation. Arouse me
from the womb of my ark. I am reborn.

Cherish me. I am fragile as belief.
Revere me. I am ancient as the oceans.
Protect me. I am newly scribed.
Lay me on your bimah. My words will rise up to meet you.
Every time you hold me, caress me with your voices,
read my words aloud, I am reborn. My words fling
out from my soul into your embrace.

My words are older than eternity. Speak my words
so I can hear you. Anoint me with your voices.
The power of voices joined in prayer
awakens the universe.

The Future

Take me to your future. Make my memories yours.
Cherish. Protect. Guard the words.

I am your Torah. Sometimes in the dark of night
all we have are words. There may be dark times.
I can guide you. Lessons are learned through the words
from study, memory, love and prayer.

Take the words of Torah to your hearts.
Explore the words in your memory.
Seek beyond the words to understanding.

Yom Ha'Atzmaut

Prayers, petitions, pleas for peace.......

I Touch the Wall

I touch the wall
The stone is surprisingly warm
in the Jerusalem sun.
My hand explores the texture
sensation of stone.

Jerusalem light fills me.
I become one
with the stones.

I am ancient
I am young
I am fragile
I am strong
I am proud

I am here.

Spaces of Time at the Wall

Silently a teardrop descends
as a note falls from between
the spaces of Jerusalem stone.
Another slips downward.

Between the spaces
of ancient solid stones
I hear-
Here O Israel,
my people weeping
through time.

Prayers, petitions, pleas for peace
praises, hopes, dreams of my people
calling, calling to G-d to
Hear, O Israel. Hear us and listen.

We are here
between the spaces
wishing, waiting, yearning
anticipating, O G-d,
an answer to our prayers.

Shavuot

We faithfully follow your commandments and desire to believe that you are with us, trusting in us, guiding us…

Shavuot

Awesome splendor engulfing Sinai. Light show
of magnificent colors. Visual dances illuminating sky.
Thunderous crescendo of sound. Ground and people trembling.
Warm cloud of smoke enveloping and weaving
round the people. Deep silence descending.
The weight of it making people sway, yearn, listen intently,
Waiting. Coming through the silence, G-d's voice heard
in the heart, in the head, in the soul.

Generations away from Sinai, I wish that I was there
enveloped by your magnificence
hearing your voice speak.
Do you know G-d how we are yearning
to hear you speak to us directly
like we are there or you are here with us again?

We faithfully follow your commandments
and desire to believe fully without hesitation or uncertainty
that you are with us, trusting in us, guiding us.
We long to hear your voice again as
we heard you, felt you at Sinai.
We wait. We pray.

Torah

G-d's book of poetry
a gift to her people.

Each Hebrew letter artistically scribed.
Beauty hidden in each graceful form.
Mystical transformation from letter
to tactile sensation of speech
to power of word.

G-d yearns for us to know, to learn
to love the words handed down to us
then look beyond the words
to understanding and belief so that each day
we awaken to a world full of
G-d's miracles, beauty, grace and poetry.

First Fruits

Shavuot- time of first fruits
ripening after harvest
wheat, barley, pomegranates,
olives, dates, figs and flowers

and people gathering
to celebrate
and give offerings of thanks
for God's goodness and fullness

in the work of the fields
has resulted in precious foods
to sustain and enrich God's people
in holiness and hope

so that now the workers and gatherers
give of themselves
can relax and listen
are ready to receive and hear the story, their story
God's story and
appreciate the laws
that guide the universe
the love of Torah
the hand of man
the arms of woman
the smiles of children
the love of story
the love of life.

Honor, Love and Remember

"Speak to the children of Israel, and have them take for Me an offering; from every person whose heart inspires him to generosity, you shall take My offering."

Parsha Terumah Exodus 25:1-27:19

And this is how you will honor me...
Men, women.
bring me gold, silver, and copper
bright blues, purples and reds
oil, spices, precious stones
whatever you desire to give, give
no more, no less
voluntarily, with joy

And this is how you will love me...
come together
to build
following my specific directions
detail by detail, precise
focused, heart and limb
with no other thought
than to serve your God

pay attention
bring your best to the task
bring your heart, your soul,
your strength to this and
every pursuit

And this is how you will remember me
take my offering of Torah
carry me with you
'see' me daily
open me

through the desert, through the cities
through wars, through times of peace
through wealth, through poverty
through sorrow, through joy
at home and away

remember how you came together to build
remember how you followed the commandments
remember how I accompanied you everywhere
remember
so you will make a sanctuary
in your home, in your heart...

Shabbat, Havdalah and Rosh Chodesh

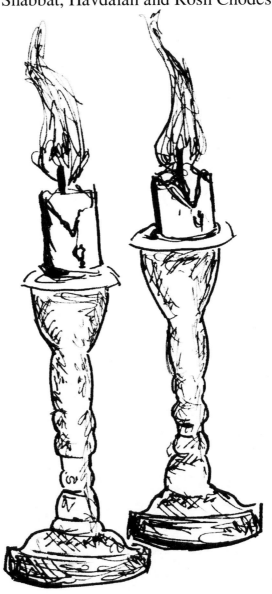

Our prayer is spoken thanking G-d for the light burning brightly in our home, in our hearts.

The Flame of Shabbat

Lighting the Shabbat candles
shielding my eyes from the brightness of
this moment, my hands circle above the flames
three times, gently drawing those I love
into my sphere of blessing.

Our prayer is spoken
thanking G-d for the light
burning brightly in our home,
in our hearts.

Shabbat gives us time to reflect.
We, who are always in motion find
an inner stillness. A distant memory of Eden
returns. Though darkness falls around us
candle light illuminates a way for us to see.

We light the candle but G-d
controls the flame. Time is suspended as
we watch the flames dance.

Prayer for Wholeness

Every week, dear G-d, you have
bestowed upon us Shabbat.
Sometimes we are so busy during the week
that we forget to feel close to you, O G-d.
We lead fragmented lives between family,
work, Judaism, extra-curricular activities. Our schedules
are so demanding that we forget to feel whole.

Dear G-d, help us to remember to reach for you.
Help us to remember to reach out to others in need.
Help us to reach inside ourselves
for time to reflect and evolve. Help us to remember
to reach for you, dear G-d.

I am just one of so many people in the world.
Sometimes I feel lost in the numbers, in this fast pace of life
lost in the should, musts and maybes
lost in my own needs, desires and worries.

I want to do more to make my life worthwhile.
I want to help others. I want to be more of who I am
and who I am meant to be. O G-d, help me to choose wisely,
focus my energy where I am needed. Help me to
see more than myself and know what is important.
O G-d, lift me, help me feel whole, Shabbat and every day.

Shabbat Light

In the glow of the Shabbat candles
I can forget traffic jams, grinding schedules
piles of laundry, office politics,
bills that are due.

For in the glow of the candles
I see the Sabbath light reflected
in my children's eyes and the warmth of my family
envelops me and gives me strength
for the coming week.

Marriage Blessing for Shabbat

(Hold your spouses' hand and look into his or her eyes)
Your words give me comfort.
Your embrace makes me feel safe.
Knowing you are there at days' end
to greet me, listen to me
gives me confidence and refreshes my spirit.

I do not take enough time
during the week to say
"Thank You" for all the wonderful things
large and small, that you do for me.

{You can insert a brief list here if desired-
e.g.: listening when I was worried,
bringing me breakfast in bed when I was sick...}

So I want to take the time now to say,
"Thank You,"
"I love you."
May our weeks together continue
to be blessed. Amen

Shabbat

I like when I look at the prayer book
and try to read the Hebrew letters.
I like when everyone stands up at synagogue
and says their own prayers, even I do!
And when I do, it feels like
I am in the prayer...

The Prayer: (by mommy)
Step forward. Step back.
We were already there, before
we started. Remind me of that
sometimes when I forget-

When I am ahead of you
and you are running to catch up-
When I am behind you, and you try to pull me faster-
When I am next to you at play-
When we are hurrying to get ready-
Hurrying to go just one more place-
Remind me:
We are already there.
We are in it. Together.
We are the prayer.

David Mark Shunfenthal © 1995 (age 6)

Havdalah

Three strands of wax intertwined-
Past, present, future.

We light the candle's wicks-
Bless the light.
Bless G-d.
Bless the flame of life.

We sanctify the Sabbath with memories.
We dip the blazing candle
into sweet wine. Moment of
darkness descends as
we separate from the sweetness
of Sabbath.

We are born into light
from darkness. We pray
to see the Sabbath Queen again.
We remember.

Rosh Chodesh, We Celebrate

Daughters of our mothers
Mothers of our daughters
Grandmothers, grandchildren
sisters, friends, wives. Come celebrate
Rosh Chodesh. Renewal.

Many phases of the moon, many phases of our lives.
Our monthly cycles are tied to the moon.
Light of the moon shines down upon us
waxing and waning in strength and determination.

We are spirited, created sacred. We give birth.
We protect and inspire.
We are creatures of renewal shining through darkness
providing light and guidance to families, friends.
We are aware of the cycles that bind us to the rhythm of life.
Monthly we celebrate
restoration, awakening, re-awakening
So that we remain strong.
So that we have courage.
So that we can support those we love.

Life cycle events

A circle of love, a world created, celebrated, and evolving under heaven.

Wedding Blessing

Earth revolving on its axis.
Seven days of creation.

Bride under the safe haven
of the chuppah circling seven times
her beloved. Their journey from this day
forward, a circle of creation, a beginning
sanctified by the blessings
of this wedding day-
(Insert date here) joined by loved ones
celebrating joyfully together.

Full cup of wine
overflowing hope, overflowing desire
overflowing devotion.
Rejoice!
(Insert names here)
drinking from the same cup-
a covenant established so that
this wedding day forms a circle
of light, from this beginning
into eternity. A circle of love,
a world created, celebrated, and
evolving under heaven.

L'Dor V'Dor
(A Baby naming prayer)

From generation to generation, we declare
G-d's praise.   Today we rejoice in celebration as we
welcome you into the covenant of Jewish family
to receive your Hebrew name.

Our heritage is a rich, colorful
cloth of many textures.   We connect
the threads of generations
remembering our ancestors
whose lives made it possible
for you to be here today.

As we imagine your future
we envision you weaving threads of Torah
family and memory into a multi-faceted
wondrous cloth which someday you
will hand down to your children.

As you grow, may the faith that you cultivate help you
in both the difficult and wonderful moments of your life.

May G-d direct you on the path of righteousness.
May your heart lead you to wise decisions.
May your family strengthen you.
May you discover the path most promising to you.   Amen

Entering the Covenant

Today we rejoice in celebration as we welcome you
into the covenant of Jewish family. The unique
relationship between G-d and the Jewish people
is expressed in the tradition that began with Abraham.

Today there is wonder, hope and promise.
May G-d be by your side in both times of joy, and times of sorrow
times of celebration and times of uncertainty.
And may family be there to guide you.

As you grow, may the faith that you cultivate
help you in both the difficult and wonderful times.
May your heart lead you to wise decisions.
May G-d direct you on the path of righteousness.
May you discover the path most promising to you.
May your life be a blessing.

The Light in Your Eyes on Bat Mitzvah Day

Here you stand beneath the Ner Tamid-
the everlasting light shining brightly in your eyes.

Thirteen years ago
I was holding you in my arms
imagining this day so many years away-
a dream of the future. Years passing quick as a
fireflies' dance or one long prayer.
Now suddenly you are here
standing beneath the Ner Tamid-
the everlasting light
burning brightly in your eyes.

Having grown beyond childhood, you stand
on the threshold of adulthood ready to discover
new horizons. Your Dad and I are proud of who
you are and who you will become. Your journey
will be full of hopes, dreams, accomplishments,
some sorrows but love will always
fill your tomorrows.

We share the miracle of this day with you- forever
etched in memory and joy, with the
everlasting light of the Ner Tamid
glowing in our eyes.

The Jewish People Gather
(on your Bar/Bat Mitzvah)

G-d spoke to the Israelites gathered at the foot
of Mt. Sinai. Each person experienced
G-d's voice in their own way:

Some heard G-d's voice
like a gentle whisper. Others heard booming
like the sound of a powerful cannon.
Some heard music and rhythm that swelled inside them
making them want to dance with joy.
Some felt G-d's voice like a soft caress.
Others felt G-d's voice as a bird's thrashing, beating
wings against their chest. Some felt transported as if
in a giant sea wave.

As we hear you speak the words of Torah, on this
your Bar Mitzvah day, it is as if we are gathered once again
at Mt. Sinai listening, experiencing G-d, each in our own way.

We hear the ancient words. Let the ancient words
guide you to the future. Open to the revelations in Torah.
We gather. We listen.
We are proud to share this special day with you.
Mazel Tov!

Broken Glass under the Chuppah

Shattered like the tablets at Sinai.
Smashed like store glass windows at Kristallnacht.
Scattered like our people during the Diaspora.
Destroyed like the Temple in Jerusalem.
Exploded like bombs on buses in beloved Israel.
Broken like our hearts when loved ones die.
Shaken like our faith during the Holocaust.

Fragmented, scattered, separated
yet we come together to celebrate the fragility
of the human heart to love. We toast the tenderness
of the human heart to hope. We applaud this new beginning.

We join together with G-d in blessing and
celebration of life as two become one
in spirit, in passion, in joy.

May the sound of breaking glass scare
away the demons and evil eye.
May the Hand of G-d bring you closer to wholeness.
May you take the broken pieces and make
them whole by your union this wedding day.
May you create Tikkun Olam with love,
hope and celebration of Life.

Love Burning Brightly

And if there are two souls who are meant for each other
and these souls find one another and their
flood of light flows together then one single
brighter light will flow stronger from their unity.

-Baal Shem Tov

Two single flames reaching
in the same direction. Warmth of the flames
embracing loved ones in the light. Separate
but together in spirit, in passion,
respectful of one another's strengths and weaknesses.

The glow of your love brings the presence of
the Shechinah- the heavenly existence
of G-d and G-dliness to earth.

May your love glow and grow over the years.
May there be more laughter than tears.
May you find in each other strength.
May your passion and joy continue burning brightly.

Adoption

One look into your bright eyes
and our future together is envisioned.
Our first hug enveloping us in a circle of love.
Holding you, hearing your heartbeat
our rhythms join together in harmony.
You fit onto our place of belonging-
our histories now joined.
Feeling your breath against us,
we flow together in song.
Family from this moment on.

Chosen
(a child adopted)

To be chosen is an honor.
Your parents were chosen for you
and you chosen for them. They dreamed
you into existence with a dream of family-
desire to nurture, love and care for you
to watch you grow, share your laughter,
encourage you to learn and listen,
wipe away fears and tears.

As a family you form a tree of life. Your roots will be
nourished with love. The trunk is the support you give each other.
The branches extend to all who care about you.

To belong to the Chosen People is to be privileged.
The Jewish family has survived and flourished throughout the
centuries. The dream of family building
roots together, sharing traditions, beliefs, love
of G-d's Torah and commandments
forms our Tree of Life.

As you become part of the Jewish family tree,
the branches extend beyond this moment into
the future. Your learning helps build your
foundation and strength. Your family and the
Jewish family are filled with pride.

Know that you are privileged
and we are privileged to share
this wonderful day with you. Mazel Tov!

Welcome to Judaism

Welcome to the Jewish tribe. You are now part of a family that has been in existence since the time of creation. You are connected to generations, going back to the beginning of time. You have acquired lots of new relatives and in Judaism, everything is relative! There are relatives everywhere (and chances are, they will all love you, try to feed you, drive you crazy and tell you stories)!

Yes, we are a people that love stories, beginning with the story of Abraham. All your relatives will have a story... that they will tell and re-tell and tell again! You have now begun to weave your story into the Jewish fabric. And it will be a great story knowing you! The Jewish people are an ancient and very wise people who also love learning. So start reading. Wise people have opinions. So when you are in a room with five Jewish people, you will get 10 opinions (and they will all be right!) That's why they invented wise guys (called Rabbis) - to moderate debates!

Don't worry though- the Jewish people have a great sense of humor. What we love to laugh at most- is ourselves. So one day when you make a silly mistake, and instead of feeling guilty, you laugh, then turn your embarrassment into a great story to exaggerate for years, you'll know for sure, you are Jewish!

The Jewish people are a proud, confident people. We have been around so long, we are sure we invented fire itself. That's why we light candles every Friday night. At Chanukah, we light more and more flames each night! But even better than that, we have an everlasting light in our synagogues whose flame burns forever. The Jewish people have been scorned, persecuted and oppressed yet the Jewish people still love to learn, laugh, eat, and tell stories. Judaism's flame continues to burn brightly- especially with people like you who choose to join the family. And wherever you travel in the world, wherever there are Sabbath candles lit, you will be welcome to join in the warmth of the light. Mazel Tov!

Prayerful Paradox

I laugh in the midst of tears.
Tears assure me I am alive.
I feel.

I cry in the midst of laughter.
Laughter is in this moment and
laughter like life ends too quickly.

In the midst of joy sometimes I feel sorrow
because I have memory of those who
are not here to share the joy.

I am joyful in the midst of sorrow
knowing I am surrounded by people who love
support and show concern for me.

I am fearful even when safe because
the future is a question to be answered.

I feel safe even when fearful because
I feel G-d's presence in the world.
The sun rises and sets. Trees blossom in spring.
Eternity is the seasons of Life.

I acknowledge your presence, O, G-d
even while I doubt your existence.
Hope resides in my yearning for you,
and a desire for wholeness.

O G-d of paradox,
dark and light, day and night
help me see you in the dark, help me hear you in my heart
help me feel you, even when I feel empty
fill me with your presence.

Remembering Loved Ones

O G-d,
Help me not to forget
those persons I once loved
who no longer live. Help me
to remember the times we laughed, loved,
talked, shared and played together.

O G-d,
Help my memories to be soft
as summer breezes, clear as spring water
not painful with tears.
May my memories be as gentle
as a hug or warm embrace.

Though the life of someone
I cherished is gone, their love lives
within me. Their legacy
of caring and compassion is part of who I am.
Their good deeds, affection, and courage
travel with me wherever I go.
In memory and spirit my loved one lives.

Yahrzeit

The flame is dancing memory
and prayer, rising in its' own rhythm,
spreading images of remembrance
of our beloved.

The yahrzeit candle burns
through day, the night.
Peace silently descends as the
light is naturally consumed.

We praise G-d who gives us life.
We, who exist in shadow
and in light.

Blessing Butterflies, Blessing Memories
(Written in memory of my mom)

You cannot call them to you
you must wait for them to come
softly, so softly memories flit around me
like colorful butterflies on a sunny, clear day.

I cannot hold them still
so delicate
wings carry dreams
remember
to hold her here in my heart
where memories flutter
here where I am beginning to heal
here where joy is a flame
that burns brightly.
Her memory is a blessing.
Let her memory be for a blessing.

I feel her hands blessing me,
caressing me with warm light of rainbows
here in my heart, she sees she is blessing me
through seasons of light and rain
flights of birds, butterflies and song
day and night, fragile and strong
hear the silent song singing
remember

Personal Reflections and Explanations

Selichot

Several days before Rosh Hashanah begins, is Selichot. Selichot is a time of song, prayers and liturgies recited in preparation for the Days of Awe (the ten days starting with Rosh Hashanah and ending with Yom Kippur). The Selichot liturgy focuses on prayers of forgiveness. I love that we have 'days of awe'- days of awakening and seeing the world with new eyes.

My Selichot poems center around forgiveness, seeking wholeness, and closeness to G-d. It is a time to search our hearts and direct our thoughts and actions towards asking for forgiveness and begin the process of teshuvah (repentance). Selichot is a time of soul searching and reflection.

The Selichot service is on a Saturday evening at the end of Shabbat. It begins after sundown and lasts well into the night. To me it is a time of inner reflection, a time to look at where I have been and remember those who came before me. It is a time also to look ahead and think seriously about ways to be better in the New Year. It is an opening to do some deep soul searching about what I need to change, and how I want to begin.

Rosh Hashana

I feel like I could write endless poems about Rosh Hashana. Rosh Hashanah literally means "head of the year" and commemorates the creation of the world and beginning of a new year. Many Jewish holidays follow the cycle of seasons. Rosh Hashana occurs in early Autumn when nature is transitioning and shedding its old self. It seems that we too are shedding our 'old selves' and opening to renewal. It is a time when we renew our contract with G-d, ourselves, our conscience, our community and our families.

I love that the Jewish New Year takes place in Autumn. Public school is just beginning. There is a crispness in the air. Colors and scents assail our senses. After the heat of summer, people are out taking walks, kids are outside playing and jumping in the leaves that are beginning to fall. There seems to be an atmosphere of hope, expectation and reflection.

During the ten days between Rosh Hashana and Yom Kippur, we are asked to open our minds and spirits to forgiveness, and reconcile any relationships that have suffered, including our relationship with G-d. We go directly to people we may have wronged and ask forgiveness. I love that Judaism asks us to go directly to a person and say we are sorry. The act of saying 'sorry' to someone eye to eye can be life changing because you must mean it. More importantly, it infers that you will not repeat the same behavior.

Part of the specialness of the Days of Awe is the sounding of the shofar, the ram's horn. The blowing of the shofar is reminiscent of what was used in the Ancient Temple. It has a unique sound that assails our senses reminding us of Jewish people of long ago. It is a startling sound demanding attention and awakening us.

At the end of the full two days of Rosh Hashana services and at our homes we share apples with honey. This symbolizes the hope for a sweet, delicious New Year. My poetry about Rosh Hashana includes poetry about creation, the startling sound of the shofar, atonement and seeking a closer relationship to G-d by appreciating the miracle of life.

Tashlich

"Tashlich" means "casting off" in Hebrew. Sins are 'cast off' and tossed into flowing water. Tiny bits of bread thrown into moving water represent our sins. As the bread is carried away in the water, our sins are carried away as well. Tashlich is usually observed on the first day of Rosh Hashana unless Rosh Hashana takes place on Shabbat, then it takes place on the second day of Rosh Hashana.

Tashlich was inspired by the words of the prophet Micah:

G-d will take us back in love; G-d will cover up our iniquities. You [G-d] will hurl all our sins into the depths of the sea. (Micah 7:19)

There is something special about a physical act of 'tossing away my sins.' It is not enough to say, "I will do better this year." Water with its' continuous flow makes us see how easily we are engaged in the flow of life but that we must interrupt the flow of bad habits, or bad deeds by casting away what is not right with our lives and what needs to be changed. We are out in the open air and the physical act of tossing gets my whole being involved in wanting to bring about change.

Shabbat Shuvah

Shabbat Shuvah is the Shabbat between Rosh Hashana and Yom Kippur. On Shabbat Shuvah we should concentrate on Torah, prayer, and repentance. Shuvah literally means "return!" We return to the best vision of ourselves and re-turn towards G-d. Again, it is time to reflect before Yom Kippur when we ask G-d's forgiveness and pray fervently that we will be written into the Book of Life for another year.

Yom Kippur

Yom Kippur is considered to be the most important holy day of the Jewish year. "Yom Kippur" means "Day of Atonement." It is a time of repentance, reconciliation and renewal. We make vows for the coming year, ask forgiveness for the sins of the previous year and pray that G-d will inscribe us in the 'Book of Life' for the coming year. We have the opportunity for T'Shuvah which means to "return." I believe it means that we return our focus to G-d and to our best vision of ourselves.

During Yom Kippur, we fast (we do not eat for 25 hours). The purpose of the fast is not punishment but focus on tefillah (prayer), increasing the intensity of prayer. We are all 'hungering' for G-d. We are focused on asking G-d to write us into the Book of Life for another year. It is a time to express forgiveness, yearning and hope from the deepest part of our hearts and souls.

I have found so many metaphors in Yom Kippur. When we fast, we are hungry- hungry for G-d, hungry for improvement of our lives, hungry for feeling safe and comforted. The sound of the shofar's blast wakes us up- we wake up to our relationship with prayer and our relationship to G-d. We bring our attention and focus back to G-d.

Sukkot

Sukkot is a seven-day harvest holiday that begins four days after Yom Kippur. After the solemnness of Yom Kippur, Sukkot is a joyous holiday. The word "Sukkot" means "booths." A sukkah is a singular structure that is built outside the home. During the forty-year period when the Israelites wandered in the desert, they lived in temporary shelters similar to the Sukkot. The holiday reminds us of that time of wandering, searching and hope under open sky. It is also a celebration of the end of the harvest season. Temporary dwellings were built in the fields during harvest time to provide shade and give shelter. After harvest it was time for relaxation and appreciation of all one has accomplished and appreciation of nature. Friends are invited to share meals in the Sukkah. Those in need are welcomed.

The sukkah must have 3 walls, be at least three feet tall, and the roof should be open to the sky. Often the top is covered with branches. The Sukkah can be covered with fruits and vegetables, leaves or Judaic images- such as Stars of David. I remember the synagogue where I grew up in Elkins Park, Pennsylvania, Congregation Keneseth Israel, had a structure that students had fun decorating with fruits we brought in and decorations we made. I always felt proud to see my fruits hanging or my drawings covering the walls.

Simchat Torah

Simchat Torah is a joyous holiday celebrating Torah. During the year, the cycle of Torah begins with Genesis and is read in sequence. On Simchat Torah, the reading is completed (with the last chapters of Deuteronomy), then immediately begins again with Genesis. It is an unending process and each time we read Torah, we are engaged in new ways and can learn something new.

On Simchat Torah, the Torah scrolls are removed from the ark and carefully handed to members of the congregation to hold. Then children and adults march or dance around the synagogue with the Torah. People kiss the Torah scrolls as they pass to show the love the Jewish people have for Torah. Often there is music, finger foods and sometimes flags that kids create that they use as they join the dancing.

My children always loved Simchat Torah because often our synagogue had a Klezmer band and there was laughing, dancing, and the opportunity to touch and see and kiss the Torah. If they were lucky they got to hold the Torah and move with it. There was also chocolate to symbolize the sweetness of Torah. Sometimes a Torah is opened fully and stretched from one end of the synagogue to the other. Now that is an extraordinary sight to see. It is a time of joy and celebration.

The poems in this section focus on how important words are to the Jewish people and the continuity of and connections of the generations of the Jewish people to Torah. L'Dor V'Dor in Hebrew means generation to generation. Torah is passed on from generation to generation. Each Torah is individually scribed by a 'sofer' who copies each letter and word of Torah onto parchment. It is copied exactly the same as it has been written for generations.

Chanukah

Chanukah a joyous celebration of a miracle. There are many metaphors in Chanukah that inspire me. That is why there are numerous Chanukah poems! There is light, which is a symbol of so many things- brightness of spirit, hope, and wisdom. The flames of the menorah, which we set in our window, is also a symbol for lighting the way through darkness. The dreidel (the Chanukah top that spins) to me dances as it turns indicating to me lightness of spirit, joy and hope. Every night for eight nights, an eight branched menorah is lit beginning with a single flame then adding one more candle each night. The second night, we light two candles, the third, three candles and continuing each night until the menorah is completely ablaze. I wondered why we light the menorah from one candle to eight candles making each night brighter. We watch that light expand which is a metaphor for G-d's light shining upon us.

The eight day holiday of Chanukah takes place in the dark of winter or towards the end of Autumn depending on where it falls on the lunar calendar. Chanukah commemorates the time when a small group of Jewish fighters, the Maccabees, miraculously defeated the powerful Seleucids (Syrian-Greeks) and were able to reclaim the Holy Temple in Jerusalem. When they went to light the Temple menorah (an ornamental seven branched candle holder), they found only one small earthen ware container holding only enough oil to last one day. Instead, it lasted eight days until new oil could be prepared under conditions of ritual purity.

It seems like such a small miracle to find one earthenware container of oil but I find in life that what often seems like a small coincidence often turns into a miracle in my life. And I love that about Chanukah. It fills my heart with joy and hope. Chanukah is a happy holiday and it does warm the winter!

Tu B'Shevat

Tu B'Shevat is the New Year for the Trees. It marks the beginning of Spring time in Israel. New buds on trees are starting to appear and the earth is ripe with possibilities. The Torah praises the Land of Israel: "A land of wheat and barley and vines and fig trees and pomegranates, a land of olive trees and honey" (Devarim 8). It is another holiday of renewal and reflection, but this time geared to the natural world and its' splendor, abundance and surprises. Blessings are focused on the fruits, the trees, and the earth.

As a tree lover, I feel a sense of wonder in Spring as buds suddenly appear on branches that yesterday looked barren, and flowers suddenly popping through the ground with vibrant colors arriving magically. It makes me want to praise G-d for these miracles and say, "thank you" for this wonder I feel.

Purim

The story of Queen Esther is to me the ultimate woman's story. I have spoken about Esther at synagogues and churches. One day I would love to write a book about Esther. Purim is the story about a young woman overcoming evil using her wits, strength of character, spirit, beauty, passion and confidence. She takes risks and prevails.

As a child, I loved Purim because it was one holiday focused on a young girl's courage. At my childhood synagogue, we had Purim carnivals and costume parades. My dearest friend Betsy and I always fought over who would dress as Queen Esther. The 'chosen' one would get to wear mom's beautiful shawl and lace, some lipstick and possibly some flowers in her hair. Beauty gets attention. Girls recognize this at an early age. It was only after several years of dressing as Queen Esther that I begin to question how beauty can save you as it felt that Queen Esther's beauty saved her.

Esther was raised in Persia by her Uncle Mordechai. She was young and stunning in appearance. After King Ahasuerus' wife refused to appear naked before the King and his drunken guests, the King banished her and decided to choose another queen. Her Uncle Mordechai tells Esther to enter the contest and become his eyes and ears within the palace. The King does not know Esther is Jewish. Mordechai advises her not to speak of her religion. Esther is chosen to become the new Queen.

When the Jewish people are in danger, Esther risks her life by approaching the King and acting graciously without greed since she has the opportunity to request anything she desires in the palace. With her wits, she saves the Jewish people. She risks power, position, her life to save her people.

The story of Purim (meaning lots) raises many ethical questions such as, "In the end, who do we cast our lots with? Do we ignore hatred and prejudice or do we speak up?" Esther probably had a very comfortable life in the palace. No one was aware of her background or relation to Mordechai. She easily could have remained 'hidden' but she chose to speak up, reveal herself and risk her life. Her religion was hidden but it was very much a part of her. She chose to be true to herself and her people.

Passover

Passover is the eight-day festival celebrated in the early spring. It is a lovely holiday that is celebrated in the home. It is similar to Thanksgiving in that family gathers around the dining room table for a meal. However, first there is the seder. Seder, means 'order.' There is a service that has an order to it and includes the story of the Jewish people fleeing slavery in Egypt, then coming to freedom.

The Haggadah is the book specifically designed for the seder. Each person at the table generally has a copy and participates in the service. There are special Passover foods. The most prominent is matzoh, the unleavened flat bread that serves as a reminder of the urgency and haste with which the Israelites fled Egypt. The slaves had no time for dough to rise, so the flat bread of matzoh was formed. Our family jokes that matzohs remind us of the burden and heaviness of slavery because after a whole week of matzoh one feels the heaviness in their gut!

It is a symbolic and metaphorical holiday in many ways. By following the rituals of Passover, it is as if we relive, celebrate and experience the freedom that our ancestors achieved.

The special Passover plate has various symbolic foods:

Maror: bitter herbs to symbolize the bitterness of slavery.

Charoses: (generally made of apples, wine, nuts and cinnamon) resembles the mortar slaves used to make the bricks.

Shank Bone: commemorates the paschal (lamb) sacrifice made the night the Hebrews fled Egypt. Parsley: represents Spring, hope and deliverance from slavery.

Salt Water: parsley is dipped in salt water to represent the tears shed while in slavery.

A Roasted Egg: symbolizes renewal and rebirth.

Several glasses of wine- makes being a large family and friend gathering much more fun and interesting although!

There is so much symbolism and metaphor in Passover. There is the symbolism on the seder plate, then the many meanings of freedom and bondage. We talk about when 'we' were slaves, so Passover feels like this happened to us recently. We can also speak about bondage to bad habits, our jobs, name brands, etc. Again, another holiday in our tradition that encourages us to embrace freedom, courage, hope and self-renewal.

Each year, I find something interesting in the Passover service that I did not see before. In the last few years, we have designed a set of questions. We take turns throughout the service to pause and choose a card with a question such as: "We can easily become slaves- to objects, money, cars, laziness, our work... How can we avoid becoming slaves?" "What journeys have you made to be where are today?" "Why are our questions so important to us?" "Why is it important to come together as family and tell and re-tell our stories, our beginnings, our family joys and sorrows and togetherness?" Passover reminds us to have stimulating conversations about the present while remembering the past. It also makes us think about whether we will all be together again the following year.

Yom HaShoah

Recently we re-visited the Virginia Holocaust Museum. It was a return visit to return to see the new Nuremberg trial exhibit. It is a very personal experience as they have actual bunkers from Auschwitz. There is an area that you must crawl through like the families that lived underground in a hold made for storing potatoes. There are the stories of families who remained in hiding and the families who hid them.   There is a boxcar that carried passengers to Concentration Camps. My husband and I were there with my college age son and we were all somewhat emotional when we left.

After we left Richmond, my husband and I returned home. It was dusk. The sun was setting when the phone rang and my friend Itka Zygmuntowicz was calling.   She is a survivor of Auschwitz. I told her where we had been and she related once again to me how she was so young when she and her family arrived starving and tired off the train in Auschwitz. Her Father was forced in one direction. Her two beloved younger siblings were forced to go another direction. Her mother turned to her and said, "Itkele, I must go with them. They need me more than you do."   She never saw her father, mother or brother and sister again.

The Holocaust museum seemed to talk about 'them' from a period before I was alive. Now suddenly speaking to Itka, it was about my friend and her family. This happened to my friend who cried for her parents, her family and chose to remember them every day and live to remember. This happened to my friend who somehow miraculously survived. This happened to my friend who created a life for herself after being close to death and undernourished. This happened to my friend who chose humanity over hatred. This happened to my friend who embraces life without bitterness or defeat.

Itka will soon be one of the last remaining Holocaust survivors and I know this makes her sad. When I hear her speak of Auschwitz, I cannot imagine what strength it took to get through each day. Yom Ha Shoah, (Holocaust Memorial Day) is a day we must all observe and think about so we keep such horror from ever happening again.

Yom Ha'Atzmaut

Yom Ha'Atzmaut is the celebration of Israel's independence which occurred on May 14, 1948. Yom Ha'Atzmaut in Israel is always preceded by Yom Hazikaron, which is the memorial day for fallen soldiers.

Israeli Independence Day is a joyous holiday celebrated in ways similar to our Independence Day. On the eve of Israel Independence Day, there are parties, singing and dancing on the streets, and fireworks. The next day there might be speeches , dancing and singing, hikes and picnics and waving of the Israeli flag.

In America, some synagogues have celebrations with music, and talks about Israel's development and future and/or eating Israeli foods. Often there are Israeli fairs with Israeli foods, music, arts and crafts or clothing from Israel. It is a nice time for the Jewish community to come together.

Shavuot

Shavuot is the anniversary of the day G-d gave Torah to the Jewish people gathered at Mount Sinai. The giving of the Torah was the most defining event in Jewish history. It was a spiritual event that formed the covenant between G-d and the Jewish people. The Jewish people were chosen to receive the Ten Commandments and pledged their commitment and love to G-d. Torah is the story, history, moral code and center of Jewish study and teachings.

The word Shavuot means "weeks" and marks the completion of the seven-week counting period between Passover and Shavuot. Shavuot in ancient times was also an agricultural festival centered around the grain harvest. I find it interesting that grains were food sustenance and Torah is sustenance for the Jewish people. On this day G‑d swore eternal devotion to us, and we pledged everlasting loyalty to G-d.

Shabbat

How does one sum up Shabbat (the Sabbath)? Shabbat is a lovely weekly holiday that we celebrate in our homes and at synagogue. We welcome Shabbat by lighting shabbat candles and reciting blessings over the candles, wine, and challah (traditional braided egg bread). My son said many years ago, Shabbat is special because it is a challah-day! After prayers, we eat the Shabbat meal which generally incudes chicken. Shabbat is relaxed time of joy and sharing, refraining from work, engaging in prayer and spending time with loved ones.

Home is "where the heart is" and the heart of Judaism is the family. Home services are special. We take time to listen to each other and talk about our week. The glow of the candles lights the room in an intimate way that pulls our family closer together and closer to Judaism. Then eating a special Shabbat meal, we take our time and focus on being present together. Rabbi Abraham Joshua Heschel and Susanna Heschel's book, *The Sabbath* is a wonderful book to read about the Jewish Shabbat.

Havdalah

Shabbat ends on Saturday night after the appearance of three stars in the sky. Havdalah is how we say "goodbye" to Shabbat. There are special blessings over the wine, fragrant spices and candle light. Havdalah means separation. We are separating holy time from everyday time, getting ready to return to work and busy schedules. We use all five senses during Havdalah prayers. We taste the wine, smell the spices, see the flame of the candle and feel its heat, and hear the blessings and songs. The fragrant spices are a symbol of the sweetness of Shabbat and the hope for a sweet week, a week of peace. The overflowing kiddush cup is also symbolic of the hope for a week overflowing in goodness. There have been many reasons given for the many strands/wicks of the Havdalah candle. Because there are several wicks the flame is brighter than everyday candle. Some say the many wicks symbolize the unity of the Tribes of Israel, or the brightness of Shabbat. We control the flame as we put out this bright light. My thought is… well, read the poem, Havdalah.

Rosh Chodesh

Rosh Chodesh is the first day of the new month. In ancient times, the day after the new moon appeared was a festival day announced with the sounding of the shofar. In more modern times it has become a woman's holiday. It is said that since the women refused to participate in the making of the Golden Calf at Sinai, Rosh Chodesh was given to the women as a reward. Some say it is also related to a women's monthly cycles and that like the moon renewing its monthly cycles, so do women.

Life Cycle Events

Baby Naming- Baby girls are generally named in the synagogue during the first Shabbat service after their birth.

Bris- Ceremony when a male baby is circumcised by the mohel (a Jewish professional specifically trained to do a circumcision) and given his Hebrew name. The ceremony symbolizes the Jewish child entering the covenant with G-d.

Bar and Bat Mitzvah- The Bar (son) and Bat (daughter) Mitzvah ceremony celebrates a child's reading from the Torah for the first time. Leading up to this event, the child has spent much time studying Jewish history, prayer, Hebrew and ethical responsibility. It is an ongoing process.

The Bar/Bat Mitzvah is public recognition of the beginning of an adolescent's journey into the Jewish community as an adult, affirming commitment to Judaism and a promise to keep the Jewish tradition alive. I will always remember looking around the synagogue at our relatives gathered from many areas of the country, friends and synagogue members gathered together to celebrate with us. I was filled with pride and joy.

The Bar/Bat Mitzvah is a marking of passage of time. It is a celebration of L'Dor V'dor (generation to generation) as well as watching the fruit of our children's long hours of study. Now many years later, we have photos from our children's B'nai (more than one) Mitzvah and I look back on the photos of relatives and friends laughing and dancing. Many of these relatives are no longer alive and I think how wonderful it was to be together for this joyful mitzvah. Once again I feel the joy and pride I felt then.

Yahrzeit- the anniversary of the death of a close relative, on which it is customary to light a memorial candle a light and recite the Kaddish (the memorial prayer). The memorial candle is a special candle that lasts for 24 hours. It always seems to me as if it brings the person's light into the room filling it in memory.

Acknowledgements
and Thank you

A huge thank you to my creative and talented daughter
Jennifer for the cover art and drawings she did for *Seasons of Prayer*.
Also, thank you to Bobbi Gorban for her time and suggestions for
artwork.

Thank you to Rabbi Aft for giving an audience at services to
my poetry. Thank you to Rabbi Bruce Aft, Rabbi Shalom Dietsch,
and Cantor George Henschel, Reverend Beth Braxton for feedback,
help editing and interesting conversations. Thank you to Ricki
Henschel for editing suggestions.

Thank you to my family who listen tolerantly to my poetry at
holidays. Thank you Dad for editing suggestions

Some of the poems in this book have been previously
published:

"Under the Chuppah." Cotner, June. *Wedding Blessings:
Prayers and Poems Celebrating Love, Marriage and Anniversaries*.
New York: Random House, Inc. 2003.

"A Baby Naming Prayer." Cotner, June. *Baby Blessings*.
New York: Harmony Books, 2002.

"Celebrating Freedom at Chanukah." Cotner, June. *Family
Celebrations*. Kansas City: Andrews McNeel Publishing, 1999.

The following poems have appeared as part of the *Circles
Within Circles: Jewish Time Frames*, a photographic/poetic
collaboration with Lloyd Wolf that explores the concept of Jewish
time (Lloydwolf.com).

Begin Again – Taschlich	Blessing Butterflies, Blessing Memories
The Light in Your Eyes on Bat Mitzvah Day	Shavuot
Under the Chuppah	Prayer for Wholeness
L'Dor V'Dor - Baby Naming Prayer	Space of Time
I Touch the Wall	The Shofar Sounds
The Flame of Shabbat	Remembering our Stories at Passover
Celebrating Freedom at Chanukah	Broken Glass under the Chuppah
Prayerful Paradox	Yahrzeit
Spaces of Time	Echoes
Coming around Again- Havdalah	

Circles Within Circles: Jewish Time Frames has been exhibited at the following places:

Jewish Community Center of Northern Virginia. Annandale, Virginia: October 2003.

UJA Federation NY Gallery. New York, New York: September 2004.

Rosen Museum. Boca Raton, Florida: January 2005.

Temple Rodef Shalom. McLean, Virginia: June 2005.

Historic 6th & I Synagogue. Washington, DC: January 2006.

Shepherd University, Shepherdstown, West Virginia: February 2009.

Futernick Gallery, Alper Jewish Community Center. Miami, Florida: October 2012.

Temple Judea Museum, Keneseth Israel, Elkins Park, Pennsylvania: February 2013.

Park Avenue Synagogue, New York, New York: March 2013.

Weinstein Jewish Community Center, Richmond, Virginia: October 2013.

Circles within Circles is currently available for exhibit: please contact Lloyd Wolf http://lloydwolf.com/ or Sherri Shunfenthal at Sherrifern@verizon.net

Sherri is available for book readings and poetry workshops. Please contact her at Sherrifern@verizon.net

Shalom

Shalom is like a circle
of friendship
of blessing
  from me to you
you to me
a wish for peace
and wholeness.

Shalom is like an open door
to walk through
when next we come together.

Shalom is the sweetness of hello
and the sadness of goodbye
but we don't really say
"goodbye"
for in our hearts we carry our knowing of each other
and memories of things learned
thoughts, ideas, events shared-
the peace fullness
of being together.

Shalom
feels so good to say.
Peace travel with you
like a friend.
Until we meet again.

About the Author

Sherri Waas Shunfenthal is a Northern Virginia poet and liturgical writer. This is her third published book of poetry. She has frequently collaborated with artists and her work has also been been published in many anthologies. Sherri also has combined her love of language, people, and poetry to form Poetry Partners, which hosts interactive poetry workshops for all ages.

Sherri's first book of poetry, *Sacred Voices: Women of Genesis Speak* (Pocol Press) was a collaboration with Washington, D.C. artist Judybeth Greene. This inspirational book has delighted people of many religious backgrounds by presenting poetry with new insight into the women of Genesis. Sherri's second book, *Journey into Healing* (Pocol Press) includes poetry, meditations and journal writing activities about women in Torah. She has spoken and presented readings at synagogues, churches, women's groups and retreats, book groups, and community colleges.

Sherri's hope is that the poems in *Seasons of Prayer* are used at your home services or are included in the liturgy at synagogues or at your special occasions. Please contact Sherri to do a book reading or poetry workshop at: Sherrifern@verizon.net or phone: 703-866-9729.